PRAISE

THE RISE OF THE REST

"*The Rise of the Rest* is a vivid and eye-opening look at the surprising acts of innovation and reinvention that are often left out of the media's spotlight. Steve Case captures the incredible stories of entrepreneurs from all walks of life who are redefining the American dream."

—**Tory Burch, executive chairman and chief creative officer of Tory Burch LLC and founder of the Tory Burch Foundation**

"In *The Rise of the Rest*, Steve Case takes us behind the scenes in cities across the country, where a new generation of innovative companies is being born and thriving. Through his up close stories of startup founders, investors, policymakers, and business leaders, Case unveils a vision of a more inclusive America, where Silicon Valley no longer has a monopoly on innovation."

—**Ray Dalio, cofounder of Bridgewater Associates and #1 *New York Times* bestselling author of *Principles***

"Steve Case played a pivotal role in getting America online, but his efforts over the last decade to create opportunity for more people in more places will be his most important legacy. I've seen firsthand the power of Rise of the Rest to empower entrepreneurs, revitalize communities, and bring people together. This captivating book will give you hope for the future of America."

—**José Andrés, chef and founder of World Central Kitchen**

"Although I represent Silicon Valley in the US Congress, I've long believed that we need to democratize innovation so we are creating tech jobs in dozens of cities, not just a few. Nobody in America has been a more visible and tireless advocate for this than Steve Case, and *The Rise of the Rest* illustrates an exciting and optimistic path forward for a more inclusive and united America."

—**Ro Khanna, member of Congress from Silicon Valley**

ALSO BY STEVE CASE

The Third Wave: An Entrepreneur's Vision of the Future

THE
RISE
OF THE
REST

How Entrepreneurs in Surprising Places
Are Building the New American Dream

STEVE CASE

AVID READER PRESS

New York | London | Toronto | Sydney | New Delhi

AVID READER PRESS
An Imprint of Simon & Schuster, Inc.
1230 Avenue of the Americas
New York, NY 10020

Copyright © 2022 by Steve Case

First Avid Reader Press trade paperback edition September 2023

AVID READER PRESS and colophon are trademarks
of Simon & Schuster, Inc.

Rise of the Rest and Revolution and all related marks are trademarks of
Revolution LLC or its affiliates and are used with permission.

For information about special discounts for bulk purchases, please contact
Simon & Schuster Special Sales at 1-866-506-1949 or
business@simonandschuster.com.

The Simon & Schuster Speakers Bureau can bring authors to your
live event. For more information or to book an event contact the
Simon & Schuster Speakers Bureau at 1-866-248-3049 or visit our
website at www.simonspeakers.com.

Interior design by Joy O'Meara @ Creative Joy Designs

Manufactured in the United States of America

1 3 5 7 9 10 8 6 4 2

Library of Congress Cataloging-in-Publication Data is available on file.

ISBN 978-1-9821-9184-9
ISBN 978-1-9821-9185-6 (pbk)
ISBN 978-1-9821-9186-3 (ebook)

To the entrepreneurs I have met in every pocket of this nation,
who are building companies, rebuilding communities,
and providing hope and opportunity for America.
This is their story.

Contents

Preface
July 4, 2026

As I write this, I am looking ahead with anticipation to a date four years away—July 4, 2026, when America will celebrate its 250th birthday. It's a milestone I think about a lot. As the chair of the Smithsonian Institution, I've been involved in planning for this celebration. And as the head of Revolution, a company investing in entrepreneurs from every corner of this great country, I've planted a stake in creating the next chapter of our nation's story.

I was just eighteen years old and fresh out of high school when I came to Washington, DC, to celebrate our nation's 200th birthday. I felt proud, excited, and inspired. I remember visiting the Smithsonian's new Air and Space Museum, which had opened that summer in celebration of the bicentennial. People gathered in DC from all across the country to commemorate our history and embrace the challenges and possibilities that lay ahead. The futurists were beginning to predict a technology revolution, but neither computers nor the internet were available to the public.

The technology revolution did happen, with America at its epicenter, and the speed with which it transformed business and society boggles the mind. America, which was just a fledgling startup nation in 1776, has continued to lead the world. Yet, in its early days, like many startups, it almost didn't make it.

There are a number of reasons for America's success over nearly two and a half centuries, but much of the credit goes to the inventors, entrepreneurs, and innovators. Their tenacity, grit, perseverance, and creativity energized a new nation and saw it through many daunting challenges.

But today, as we head toward our big 250th birthday, some are asking whether that spirit is still alive. According to a Pew Research study, a majority of Americans are pessimistic about the future. They worry about the widening gap between rich and poor, a declining standard of living for the middle class, and the threat to jobs posed by automation. This demonstrates a disconnect between two different visions of progress.

Some pundits have concluded that America's best days may be behind it. For them, the challenges within the country and the competitive threats around the globe are a harbinger of doom. I understand the concerns but see them as more of a warning—a wake-up call that we must heed.

The strategic questions are clear: How do we continue to lead, inventing the technologies that can enable the industries of the future to flourish? And how do we figure out ways to create more opportunity, for more people, in more places, so the United States can develop a more inclusive innovation economy?

Part of the reason our country is so divided right now is that many people feel left behind in the new economy. When tech innovators in Silicon Valley boast about disruption, many in the rest of America see job losses in their communities. And while it's true that new technologies often result in job losses, as tech solutions can indeed enable more to get done by fewer people, it's also true that new business startups are the biggest job creators. We must be more thoughtful about backing startups in every part of the country to offset inevitable job losses with new opportunities and help more people participate in a growing economy.

People around the world are still largely envious and respectful of America. But that admiration is not a birthright. It must be earned continually. If we lose our way, it probably won't be because a rising power like China undermines us, although that is of course a risk. More likely it will be because we undermine *ourselves*.

This might sound like a familiar theme coming from me. In my first book, *The Third Wave: An Entrepreneur's Vision of the Future*, published in April 2016, I sounded a similar warning, that America was at risk of losing its lead as the world's most entrepreneurial nation. That warning came months before the 2016 election, but the depth of the chasm between the tech world and the rest of the country was only fully revealed with the election of Donald Trump, which surprised many people on the coasts—though not most of the voters in the rest of the country.

The instinct of some to look toward Washington to fix the dysfunction in our nation seems misguided, especially when the two parties are resistant to working together—making collaborative, nonideological approaches to solving problems increasingly rare.

Government can—and *must*—play a role, but it's clear that we can't rely solely on government to fix something that's wrong in the marrow of our communities. We need to lead from the grassroots, and we especially need the nation's entrepreneurs to step up. My goal is to see that entrepreneurial dynamism happening all across the country, so we can create jobs, hope, and opportunity everywhere, and build a brighter shared future for America.

Before he died in 2007 at the age of eighty-four, futuristic novelist Kurt Vonnegut expressed dismay at the state of the nation and suggested that the country could use a new cabinet position: the secretary of the future. He was right, and it's still true. We need an all-hands-on-deck effort to position America for the future.

So, what can we do to be sure the United States *does* lead? That question has been at the heart of my work over the past decade and is the underlying theme of this book. The Rise of the Rest means just what it says: a way to lift the prospects of *the rest* of the nation—those who live and work outside the coastal tech centers in California, New York, and Massachusetts. Currently, 75 percent of venture capital for startups flows to those three states, with the rest of the country left to fight it out for the remaining 25 percent.

Our effort to level the playing field begins to bring those who have been left behind into the center of the action. The deep anxiety, resentment, and despair in some parts of the country can be addressed in part through the economic and social engines of entrepreneurial ecosystems. The revival of American cities is the practice of the art of possibility—the ability to see problems as opportunities, and focus not on what might go wrong but on what can go right. It's not just talking about the pitfalls but illuminating the vision—saying, "What will this look like if it succeeds?" Just as they helped build America in its first two centuries, entrepreneurs can once again help to lead the way.

AT HOME IN THE LAND OF PROMISE

Our nation has always called on every generation to invent the future anew, while drawing on the wisdom of the past. I come from America's fiftieth state, Hawaii, which gained admission on my first birthday. So, in a sense I got here by the seat of my pants. I consider myself privileged to have been born in a place infused with a unique spirit, history, and culture.

Hawaii was very different from the mainland and had once been on the pioneering edge of our hemisphere. As a series of islands, with limited interaction with the rest of the world, it had to be self-sufficient and embrace novel approaches to life's problems. Hawaiians were innovative by necessity, whether it was inventing new ways to move water to grow food or creating different strategies for navigating the seas.

That focus on doing things better also inspired people to move to Hawaii, including my great-grandparents, who arrived there more than a century ago, energized by the prospect of being pioneers in a new land.

But for me Hawaii was also a cautionary tale. When I was growing up in the 1960s and '70s, the economy was in upheaval. An overreliance on agriculture as the primary industry had led to massive job losses, as global competition in crops such as sugar and pineapple intensified. Thankfully, Hawaii was able to pivot to tourism, and the launch of the jumbo jet led to a wave of economic vitality. Workers were retrained to move from farms to hotels and restaurants. The tourism industry brought fresh opportunities, but also a new set of challenges. Many lamented the way large areas of formerly pristine and beautiful land were transformed into concrete jungles. Worried about the changes, people often became cautious and risk-averse—less open to change.

By the time I graduated from high school in 1976, I was eager to set off and seek opportunities that I didn't think existed for me at home. I wanted to lean into the future—indeed, I hoped to play a small role in *creating* the future.

That desire became the core idea for America Online, which I cofounded in 1985. The goal was to get *all* of America online. In the early days of the internet, there was an elitist notion that this important new technology was best left in the hands of a select few. The internet started as a Cold War government technology—it was a network designed to be resilient so it could withstand a nuclear attack. It only gradually reached the broader public. Even then it was not being widely used; until 1990 access was restricted to government agencies and educational institutions. AOL, promoting grassroots access for everyone, was ahead of its time.

It could get lonely out on the internet frontier in the 1980s. Consider this: When we started AOL, only 3 percent of Americans were online, and those early adopters were only online an average of one hour a week. It wasn't exactly a groundswell!

Given that, America Online was a bold name. I thought of it as aspirational, but we had a lot of convincing to do. There were times when we were on the brink of failure because a business model built on an unexplored future was seen as extremely high-risk. However, I never doubted that we were creating a medium that would change the world.

Our challenge was to help people visualize it, experience it, and believe in it. We had to show them that the internet could be life changing—not just technology for technology's sake. We promised that a whole new world was opening up for them, even if they could not quite see it yet. And what excited me the most was knowing that we were providing access to people, ideas, and commerce that had previously only been available to a few.

My experience building America Online and evangelizing the benefits of the internet across the nation proved invaluable in 2014 when I launched Rise of the Rest, an initiative at my investment firm Revolution, designed to promote regional entrepreneurship—helping startups emerge and scale throughout the country. The challenge of creating jobs and opportunity is quite different from building on-ramps to the internet, but the underlying purpose is similar. Part of my passion at AOL was the effort to give everyone access to the promise of the internet. Rise of the Rest is about providing access to the rewards of technology. What if everyone had an equal chance to create and thrive—no matter where they live or what their background? Which brings us to the story I'm telling in this book.

My early experiences growing up in Hawaii and starting AOL in the Washington, DC, region helped prepare me for what I would find in many of the Rise of the Rest cities we visited. Just as Hawaii was sometimes slow to embrace new ideas, I found starting a new company in DC to be quite difficult. In the 1980s DC was still a government town. Startups were rare, and venture capital was virtually nonexistent. Convincing people to leave large, stable companies to join a fledgling and risky startup was a tough sell. I felt like a fish out of water once again, living in a place that was focused more on preserving the status quo than embracing the future.

When I started Rise of the Rest, I wanted to make it easier for the next generation of entrepreneurs to found companies in places like DC, or anywhere else in the nation they happened to be. I hoped that they'd have more access to capital, be better able to attract talent, and build companies in communities that believed in them and truly wanted them to succeed.

From the outset it was important for Rise of the Rest to engage with startups and communities on the ground—not to be an abstract organization directing things from afar. I had experienced the value of hometown events when we were launching AOL and decided to replicate the idea. We borrowed a strategy from our home base of DC and procured a large coach bus, in the manner of a political campaign, although this was a very different kind of campaign. We painted it red and stamped "Rise of the Rest Road Trip" on the side, along with the names of the cities for each tour. You couldn't miss it, which was the point.

The bus tour is built on the quintessential American tradition of road trips. Some thought it was a great piece of theater, and while it did help us get press attention, it was much more than that. We became a rolling connector and accelerator, inviting local entrepreneurs onboard to talk to high-level investors, corporate CEOs, influential government officials, and our own team—all wanting to listen to what they had to say. Entrepreneurs don't usually get access to such top-echelon guides and investors. And investors from the coastal tech hubs don't usually get a front-row seat to the innovation that's happening in the heartland.

We designed the arc of each tour to be five cities in five days, effectively sixty hours of cultural immersion, programming, and making connections. Once the bus rolls into town, it commands attention, and over the years it has become identifiable as a sign that innovation is happening in a community. The tour events are built around local startups, and the days are packed. We get off the bus and begin with a big breakfast event at an iconic location, attended by entrepreneurs, local and state officials, organization leaders, investors, and allies from across the state who are invested in the success of startup ecosystems. Sometimes we're joined by celebrities or by governors and US senators. Then we do what we call a startup ecosystem crawl. That means going out and experiencing everything firsthand. It's not just the startups themselves that interest us but the whole environment around them. We try to highlight all the other ecosystem players. Sometimes that means going to a university that's doing groundbreaking work. Sometimes it's a more established local business that is supporting startups. Sometimes it's an accelerator—a local organization and workspace for startup businesses. Often, we visit those pre-IPO startups that have risen, and demonstrate what's possible when you back entrepreneurship.

At the end of each tour, we hold a pitch competition for ten local startups—the finalists culled from hundreds of entries—and award the winner a $100,000 investment. The competitions usually attract very large cheering crowds and are high-octane finales. Then we get back on the bus and move to the next city. But our visits are more than a quick in and out. Every visit is backed by six months of work before we get there and six *years* of work after we leave. The commitment extends far beyond the tour.

Between 2014 and 2020 (when we paused the physical visits during the pandemic), we completed eight bus tours, visiting forty-three cities, and traveling eleven thousand miles, to every region of the country. The people we've met on the tours now serve as an incredible network of investors, founders, and ecosystem builders passionate about garnering support for their cities. We stay in close contact through regular calls, city visits, and Rise of the Rest summits and convenings. This allows us to continue to understand the unique challenges and opportunities that exist for founders in cities across the country, and enables our team—led so ably by managing partners David Hall and Anna Mason—to monitor for the next potential breakout companies.

We knew going into the Rise of the Rest bus tours that there was a level of stagnation in parts of the country. But we didn't accept the conventional wisdom that jobs would inevitably continue to drain out of the industrial Midwest or the South and that nothing could be done to stop it. This wasn't blind faith on our part. A change was already happening. Beneath the surface, dozens of American cities had already started the process of developing startup ecosystems, and they now needed a boost in organization and capital to propel them into long-term success.

It was a similar dynamic to the one I encountered with AOL. I remembered those difficult early days, when few saw the value of the internet, and most were certain it would have limited appeal. They were right for a decade, as internet adoption grew slowly and it proved hard for AOL and other early internet companies to get traction. But then it hit a tipping point, and almost overnight the mentality shifted from nobody caring about the internet to everybody wanting to be on it.

The early Rise of the Rest experience gave me a sense of déjà vu, and I was driven once more by my desire to prove the doubters wrong. (Yes, I, like many entrepreneurs, do my best work when told something is not possible. Growing up, it didn't take my parents long to figure out that the best way to get me to do something was to tell me it couldn't be done.) But it wasn't just about proving a point. More fundamentally, it was about backing entrepreneurs everywhere, and in the process leveling the playing field of opportunity.

Today, as I write this, there is an explosion of startup ecosystem development in dozens of cities—a wonderful and largely untold story. From Seattle to Phoenix to Salt Lake City to Dallas to Denver to Miami and all points in between, startups are reimagining cities. The new guard is reviving declining iconic places like Detroit and Pittsburgh, once great centers of innovation that fell on hard times. They are electrifying smaller cities like Chattanooga and Columbus with tech innovation in critical industries such as insurance, health care, and transportation. They are energizing classic heartland cities like Kansas City, Green Bay, Omaha, and St. Louis with a renewed focus on the future. And they are cracking the equity code, engaging diverse populations in cities like Atlanta, Baltimore, and Tulsa in the opportunity to rebuild America.

It's often a "pinch me" experience on the bus, as entrepreneurs interact with people—some of whom are their heroes—and have inspiring conversations. Sometimes we talk about the tour as putting kerosene on the fire—trying to create a tipping point and instilling a we-can-do-it ethos that inspires a startup movement that lives on for many years to come.

After we visited Albuquerque, Mayor Richard Berry wrote to me: "I just want to let you know that your visit to Albuquerque changed our city. It was the spark that we needed. You believed in us, and we started believing in ourselves."

Rise of the Rest has shown us that new job creation can happen everywhere, and it is now happening in countless communities. But it has to be approached in a strategic way. You can't create lots of new jobs unless you create new companies, and you can't create new companies unless you create a culture to nurture startups. That means also winning the battle for talent and capital and building communities that support entrepreneurs.

When we look back at this moment in America's history, all the complicated challenges that face our country may be summarized most simply as a battle between optimists and pessimists. I am an optimist. This book explains why. It is dedicated to the extraordinary entrepreneurs, innovators, and change-makers I have met on our road trips. *The Rise of the Rest* is their story. And the story is just beginning.

In many ways, the Rise of the Rest is the answer to the question of whether America can maintain its lead in the world. It's impossible to read these stories and not be filled with a sense of excitement about the future and an anticipation that, if we stay the course, there will indeed be more to celebrate in 2026, when the startup called America turns 250.

PART ONE

PLACE MATTERS

ONE

On the First Tour

When we were gearing up for our first Rise of the Rest bus tour in 2014, it seemed only natural to choose Detroit, the Motor City, as the initial stop. It's a city steeped in the history of American innovation, now striving mightily to regain its greatness.

One hundred years ago Detroit was the Silicon Valley of its day. The tech stars then were called Car Guys. Everybody wanted to be part of the car revolution, to have a role in creating the automotive wonder that sat in almost every driveway in the country and fueled an economic and social transformation for generations.

The birth of the car industry was an exhilarating time. There were originally one hundred auto-related startups vying to break through. A few rose to dominate, and eventually leadership settled into the Big Three—General Motors, Ford, and Chrysler. They knew what customers wanted and they built the cars that would fulfill their needs and fantasies. The American automobile was wrapped up in ideals of technology, speed, romance, convenience, and the freedom of an open road.

Then the wheels came off. By the 1990s, Detroit had lost its mojo. Corporate complacency and stiff international competition were the triggers, and the American collapse just kept getting worse. Automakers, along with the network of companies feeding into the industry, started going out of business and shedding jobs, and this once vibrant city became a shadow of its former self. In half a century it lost 60 percent of its population. Just a year before our bus pulled in, Detroit had declared bankruptcy.

But I believed that Detroit was poised for revival. As I saw it, all the ingredients were in place for it to rise again. For one thing, America was rooting for its return. That confidence was paired with the advance of a generation of startups leveraging digital technologies to create new opportunities, while also reviving old industries, including the auto industry.

Dan Gilbert, the founder of Quicken Loans, has played a pivotal role in leading Detroit's revival. Back in the 1980s, Dan and his brother Gary founded Rock Financial, a mortgage lender, in Detroit, their hometown. They sold it to Intuit in 2000, and Intuit renamed it Quicken Loans. Two years later, Dan led a group of investors in buying back Quicken Loans, and he became chairman and the majority shareholder. He built it into an extremely successful company, located in an office park in a Detroit suburb.

As the company expanded, Dan began to look for more office space, and he started to think about how to help his hometown, which was really struggling. He decided to move Quicken Loans and its 1,700 employees to downtown Detroit, as a sign of faith in the city. But he did more than that. He began buying vacant buildings in the downtown area with the idea of revitalizing it. Dan ended up acquiring more than one hundred buildings, many of which had been abandoned as companies left the city and moved to the suburbs. He was tapping into a turning tide. Companies were recognizing that they needed talent, including young employees with fresh perspectives, and a lot of those people didn't want to live and work in the suburbs. They wanted to live in cities, where they could walk to work, where all their needs were conveniently situated, and where the social and cultural arena was more diverse and appealing to them. This reawakening led to a reversal of fortune as companies that had left cities began to return so they could win the battle for talent.

Those empty buildings that Dan Gilbert bought when few others were interested suddenly started filling up. Downtown Detroit became a magnet for talent and the epicenter of the city's startup community.

Dan had a message to the nation about Detroit: "Don't give up on us, we're going to fight to become a great city again." Once he opened the door to new possibilities, he found that Detroit had a remarkable roster of advocates from both the public and the private sectors, all eager to do their part. These included local business and philanthropic leaders, as well as the three big automakers, GM, Ford, and Chrysler. Mayor Mike Duggan, elected in 2013, was dedicated to urban renewal and had a history of reviving struggling businesses. A popular mayor, in his third term as of this writing, he has been at the forefront of efforts to make Detroit a leading city of the future. He recognizes that support for entrepreneurs and innovation is a key component of that vision.

When Rise of the Rest was planning its first tour, Dan enthusiastically convinced us that Detroit had turned the corner and was back on the path to greatness. He was our high-energy tour guide throughout the day. One of our visits was to Shinola Manufacturing. Shinola has an interesting story, showing that sometimes the discovery of innovators can be serendipitous.

My longtime friend, partner, and investor Ted Leonsis had read an ad about a classic watchmaker dedicated to creating world-class manufacturing jobs in Detroit. Ted was so interested in the concept that he went out and bought a watch and ended up engaging with the salesperson about Shinola's mission to lift up Detroit workers. "It was evident that the sales associate was truly in love with the company, its quality manufacturing, and the creation of good-paying, quality jobs in Detroit," Ted reported when he told me about Shinola. He praised Shinola for its authenticity and the power of its mission. Almost counterintuitively in the smartphone era, there was a market for high-quality, curated products like the timepieces Shinola was manufacturing.

When we were planning our Detroit trip, Ted asked me to put Shinola on the schedule, pitching it as a promising brand that could serve as a "gateway to luxury for the new generation that cares so deeply about the source of their goods and food." He analyzed this younger generation as wanting to have an honest connection to the things they wear and eat. "A sense of place—especially here in America—is of more significance to young people, and I also believed this could be a great growth company and a very successful business."

We put Shinola on the schedule and met its founder, Tom Kartsotis. Tom is a quiet, behind-the-scenes craftsman who shies away from publicity. As we toured the facility, we recognized that there was indeed something special going on. I thought the vision had a touch of genius grounded in the psychology of the American consumer. People would be drawn to a company that was fighting for America. Wearing the watch would be a patriotic gesture, symbolizing the revival of the nation's heartland and its beloved city of Detroit. Our visit later led to our Revolution Growth fund investing in Shinola.

Toward the end of our Rise of the Rest tour day in Detroit, Dan and I sat down together for a fireside chat at Grand Circus, a tech hot spot in the heart of the city.

Detroit, Dan said, "truly is an incredible place, but you really have to get here. My words don't give it justice. It doesn't matter who we take through the tour, whether it's Steve Case or Madonna, they're wowed because it's not their expectation."

I seconded that observation. Detroit had a chance to symbolize a particular American resolve to do something, not because it's easy but because it's hard. "There are lots of people here because they want to be part of the next era of Detroit," I said that day. "The whole country can play a role in the continuation of the American story. Detroit's last half-century has not been good, but what's happening now is a rebuilding of hope and optimism."

I emphasized that these efforts were bolstered by the growing recognition on the part of big companies like Quicken Loans that the best way to rebuild the community—and attract the millennial talent that they also need to succeed—is to partner with entrepreneurs who have innovative ideas. In this way, established companies can help startups succeed, and startups can help established companies remain relevant, all the while creating jobs, hope, and opportunity in the communities they care so much about.

SPARKING OPPORTUNITY

When we decided to hit the road with our Rise of the Rest bus, we wanted to go deep into each city we visited, to really understand what was happening, to use our platform to shine a spotlight on people and ideas, and to drive more collaboration. We also wanted to attract local press attention, so the stories of startups would get more focus. That led us to end each day with a pitch competition, with promising entrepreneurs competing for a $100,000 investment.

More than one hundred startups applied to enter our first pitch competition in Detroit. The winner was Stik.com, a professional services review site, which was an inspiring heartland revival story. The founders, Harvard grads Nathan Labenz and Jay Gierak, started Stik in 2010 in San Francisco. Two years later, they brought the company to their hometown of Detroit. Their reasoning for the relaunch was in sync with the Rise of the Rest message: you don't have to be in Silicon Valley to make it, and in fact sometimes other cities can be more welcoming for your company.

For Nathan and Jay, the disadvantages of Silicon Valley outweighed the advantages. Fierce competition for talent and capital and the environment of frequent turnover made them question their long-term potential. Detroit offered more stability. The talent there was almost as strong, and there was less competition and better access. Teams were more committed to the long haul. Coming home to family and friends was a big part of the appeal. When they won the Rise of the Rest pitch competition, it was the icing on the cake.

But this wasn't a fairy-tale story. Shortly after Stik's win, calamity struck. Because of abuses alleged in firms such as

Cambridge Analytica, it was announced that the social media data that many companies, including Stik, had been relying on would be inaccessible in just one year. Nathan was sitting in bed on a Saturday morning scrolling through the business news when he read the news flash. He woke his wife. "I think we're going to have to shut down the business," he told her.

"What?" She was alarmed.

"They're not going to give people access to social connection data anymore," he explained. That surely would be the end of Stik, as its business model would be decimated.

"We were faced with this really weird situation," Nathan recalled. "We'd just won the Rise of the Rest competition. We had a great story to tell, but we had to transition into a different story."

When the Stik team had a chance to think about it, they realized their only choice was to pivot—under duress. They had a little money left in the bank, and the credibility they'd gained from the Rise of the Rest pitch victory, to reinvent themselves. They had just one year to get it done.

"This was where being a Detroit company was an advantage," Nathan said. "In Silicon Valley there's an attitude of 'fail fast and shut it down.' But Detroit was still new to the creation of startups, and people were more geared to fight for them. If we shut down, that would mean jobs lost. So, we fought on, and the community rallied around us to help."

They began to explore promotional concepts that would support small businesses and landed on the idea of creating customized video tools—video marketing for everybody—a new company that would ultimately be relaunched as Waymark in 2017.

The road to relaunch was rocky, and they almost failed a few times. They were testing the market and barely making it. They weren't sure if they had a chance or if they were kidding themselves, so they set a goal: four months to get one thousand paying customers. "If we couldn't do that," Nathan said, "we'd have a 'come to Jesus' moment and possibly shut the whole thing down." The next months were frantic as they worked their database, went through a nail-biter gaining acceptance, and hoping the orders would come in. At the end of three and a half months, they passed the one thousand mark and breathed a sigh of relief—briefly. "It was total insanity," he said. "We now had to create one thousand campaigns."

Nathan likened the experience to a scene from his favorite movie, *The Three Amigos*. "When they break into El Guapo's fortress, the woman asks them, 'What is your plan?' And he says, 'First we break into El Guapo's fortress.' And she says, 'And that you've done. Now what?' And he says, 'Well, we didn't really expect the first part of the plan to work, so we didn't think much about what we were going to do next.' And that's where we were. We actually got to a thousand customers, but now we had to figure out not only how to get more but how to actually deliver. And we were still burning money."

Looking back on those days from a point in late 2021 when the company finally started making a profit, Nathan thinks about the advice he'd give to other startups, based on his struggles. "How do you succeed in a startup? You just keep trying until you succeed," he reflected. Nathan doesn't consider the company completely out of the woods yet. It's a long haul, which is typical.

For a long time, Silicon Valley has perpetuated the myth of startups being the road to easy riches. All that's needed is a great idea. The reality is far different. About 90 percent of all startups fail—good idea or not. Founders like Nathan lead 24/7 work lives for years keeping their companies afloat and eking out profits before reaching more stable success.

HOW TO IDENTIFY STARTUP POTENTIAL

From this first bus outing, we developed a set of criteria that we use to evaluate entrepreneurs for the pitch competitions and for other investments. We begin with three questions:

Why me?
Why now?
Who cares?

At its heart, "Why me?" is the identity question. There's a temptation to define one's startup in comparison to others. Answering the "Why me?" question forces founders to stand on their own and make the case for themselves and their company. What's original about it? Does it make sense as a business? Does it meet a felt need? Is it venture backable? Can it scale quickly?

These are all critical pitch questions, and every startup founder has to have a pitch. Eric Schmidt, the iconic business entrepreneur and former chairman of Google/Alphabet (and an investor in Rise of the Rest), has an exercise he does with early-stage startups. He tells them, "Give me your pitch. I am your first customer." Often these early founders stumble when it comes to selling that "first customer" and fail to articulate their value in a clear and tangible way.

"Why now?" is a timing question. It might be the most brilliant idea in the world, but if it's too soon for the market, and not ready for consumer or enterprise adoption, or the infrastructure isn't there, it might not survive long enough for it to fly.

It is often said that timing is everything, and that became clear during the pandemic. Some businesses failed, but many flourished. Utah-based Neighbor accelerated its growth by offering a more convenient and affordable alternative to self-storage. Neighbor gained early momentum, but things really took off during the pandemic—quintupling its revenue and demand. The reason was obvious: more people were moving, and a lot were going to temporary housing. They needed to store their stuff. In addition, the commercial real estate market was crashing in several cities, and landlords and owners were left with a high inventory of empty spaces. Neighbor worked to set up storage arrangements so there would be some income generated from empty properties. Neighbor went on to raise more than $50 million in Series B funding *during* the pandemic.

"Who cares?" asks about the market. We want to encourage innovation in important aspects of our lives and disrupt—and reimagine—the largest industries in the world. We are looking for entrepreneurs who seek to solve big problems and seize large opportunities. When we make an investment in a startup, we want to be sure the battle is worth fighting, and the mountain is worth climbing.

DOUBLING DOWN

When we were putting together our first Rise of the Rest tour in 2014, we didn't really know what we were getting into. The cities we selected for that first tour—in addition to Detroit, we toured Pittsburgh, Cincinnati, and Nashville—each had interesting histories, but less certain futures. It was not clear what we'd find when we hit the road and rolled into town.

It didn't take long for us to realize we were on to something. First in Detroit and then in the other cities, we found tenacious communities determined to fight their way back to relevancy. Just as entrepreneurs fight for their startups to survive and eventually succeed, we met a wide range of people in each of the cities who had decided to do what they could to change the trajectory of their cities. No more would people settle for the status quo and hope that existing anchor companies would continue to carry the economic load. That was eventually a losing strategy. Instead, these communities were focused on seeding new companies that could create growth and momentum in the cities they loved.

We learned that there is real value in showing up. In every city we were well briefed on the dynamics, the challenges, the opportunities, and the key movers and shakers. But that was just words on paper. Showing up, and meeting people face-to-face, in their cities, opened our eyes to what was really happening and strengthened our connection to and affection for each community we visited. Our interactions, on and off the bus, were meaningful and catalytic.

The pace of our bus tours was sometimes exhausting, but we fed off each other's energy and sense of hope. People seemed to really appreciate that we were there and respected what we were trying to do. One after another our hosts used our visit to shine a spotlight on what was working and pull more people and companies into their efforts to create stronger startup communities. They had been doing the work, often under the radar. Our presence lifted those efforts.

I want to be clear. Rise of the Rest did not "rescue" these cities. They rescued themselves. By the time we arrived, a lot of good things were happening. We just came along and championed their efforts.

The bus tours were an important first step, but we knew we had much more to do if we were going to have any hope of jump-starting more systemic change. Our team identified the local venture investors in each city and started connecting them with other investors in other cities, to build a network of regional venture capitalists that worked to find and build startup potential and engineer thriving startup ecosystems.

It's all about making connections, which is pretty much the same thing I was doing early in my career when I cofounded AOL. That was about building networks too—communications networks to facilitate connections, and community features like chat rooms to connect people. With Rise of the Rest, I'm back in the network-building business. The only difference is that at AOL I was working to level the playing field in terms of information and education, and now it's about capital to fuel ideas, job creation, and transformation in communities.

Within a year of launching Rise of the Rest, the idea was growing that we had to do more if we were serious about serving these communities and companies. The $100,000 pitch competitions were a good start, but they weren't enough. Our investment goals were expanding beyond the tour competitions to other companies we met on the road.

The communities saw the need as well. I remember sitting in a diner in Philadelphia in 2015 as part of our Rise of the Rest tour. Then-mayor Michael Nutter was speaking about the promise of revival in his great historic city. As he finished speaking and was leaving the room, he stopped beside me and leaned in. "Steve, you've got to stay engaged," he whispered. "We must do more here. We've got to think about an enduring way to create a structure that lives on, long after you and your team depart." There was such urgency in his voice. I knew he was right.

We started hearing the same thing wherever we went. It was the most consistent challenge in the Rise of the Rest communities—that they didn't have the connectivity or the capital to do what they wanted to do. They were grateful for our visit, for the connections we forged and the publicity we brought to their efforts. But they also needed a serious buy-in from the investment community.

In 2017 Revolution launched the first $150 million Rise of the Rest Seed Fund to catalyze more investment in rising cities. Notably, one of the first people to invest in the fund was Dan Gilbert.

Our involvement helps credential companies, making it easier for them to attract other investors. It raises their visibility as they seek to attract talent, and it connects them with potential customers and startup evangelists in their cities. By creating a national network of both investors and entrepreneurs, we're able to begin building the type of network density that has been such a powerful contributor to Silicon Valley's success.

We assembled an impressive group of iconic entrepreneurs, investors, and business leaders to join us, including Jeff Bezos, Tory Burch, Howard Schultz, Mike Bloomberg, David Rubenstein, Jeff Vinik, Roger Ferguson, Sara Blakely, Ray Dalio, Sheila Johnson, Mike Milken, James Murdoch, Eric Schmidt, Henry Kravis, Kevin Plank, Joe Mansueto, Meg Whitman, Jim Breyer, Ted Leonsis, Bill Lewis, Josh Harris, Romesh Wadhwani, John Doerr, Byron Trott, Dan Gilbert, Brad Smith, Reid Hoffman, and members of the Walton and Koch families.

Over the years, the contributions of our investors have been game changers, not just in providing capital but also in establishing credibility. When others see that investors believe in the Rise of the Rest thesis—that the next great wave of companies can come from outside Silicon Valley—it increases our momentum.

Since we launched the first fund, followed by a second $150 million fund in 2019, we've invested in more than two hundred companies in more than one hundred cities. Through it all we're always looking for great entrepreneurs and great founders. We're dedicated to building disruptive companies to solve big problems.

Meanwhile, the bus tours created a certain momentum of their own. They became a way of bringing people together and giving them a road map for pursuing their dreams. Winning the competition had tangible meaning beyond the $100,000 prize. It de-risked the companies that won, and legitimized them, as they sought to hire people and raise money. They weren't just viewed locally as risky fly-by-night, likely-to-fail startups. They were suddenly credentialed, and were increasingly perceived to be real companies that had real prospects, because they had been validated by a national brand.

We also found, much to our delight, that the other startups in the pitch competitions often benefited, even when they didn't win. Frequently, they'd let us know that they attracted new investors, or secured new customers, because of Rise of the Rest. We heard a common refrain: "Thank you for putting us on the stage and giving us a shot."

WHEN INVESTORS BELIEVE IN YOU

One of the most gratifying parts of being engaged with startups in the heartland is that there are so many unexpected stories, when the most unlikely ideas turn to gold. Greg Schwartz's Detroit adventure was such a story. It began as he was literally on his way out of the state, headed west. Plane tickets to California had been purchased. His wife was looking at houses there. A Detroit native, Greg had been working the entrepreneurial circuit for a few years. He was about to exit a company and had accepted a job offer in Silicon Valley when he got a call from Dan Gilbert, an investor in his previous startup, who wanted to talk to him. "When you're in Detroit and Dan Gilbert wants to talk to you about starting a new company, you take that meeting," he said.

They met at Dan's office in downtown Detroit. Dan got right to the point. "Greg, don't move to California," he said. "Don't take that offer. Let's start a new company together." He had an idea, which at first sounded strange, but as they talked, Greg became more excited. "The idea grew out of the concept of leveraging stock market mechanics in an entirely new form of commerce," Greg explained. "There are tremendous efficiencies in the way that the world's financial exchanges operate, and a lot of those attributes are absent when you think about traditional consumer goods marketplaces." Dan's concept involved taking some of those attributes and combining them with a consumer goods experience, to get the best of both worlds—unlocking economic opportunity for sellers and bringing visibility, trust, and authenticity to buyers.

Their conversation took place on a Friday evening. By Monday morning Greg had canceled his move and started working. It was a "leap of faith," but it was irresistible to have this opportunity in Detroit.

In choosing a product to launch with, Dan, the father of four boys who were obsessed with cool sportswear, suggested sneakers. Greg looked down at his own feet. "I was wearing the one pair of brown loafers that I owned at the time, and I said, 'I think, Dan, you might have the wrong guy.'"

Dan laughed, but they found their secret weapon a couple months later, with "sneakerhead" Josh Luber as part of the founding team. That year Dan, Greg, and Josh launched StockX—"the stock market of things"—a secondary market for high-demand hot items. Our Rise of the Rest fund was among StockX's initial investors. There was also a "cool" factor that attracted celebrity investors such as Eminem and Mark Wahlberg. These celebrities lent credibility in the national sneaker market.

When I first visited StockX in 2015, Dan took me downstairs to a basement room in the Quicken Loans headquarters building, where a dozen or so people were working on the fledgling idea. Five years later, StockX employed more than one thousand people, was worth more than $1 billion, and hired Scott Cutler, the former EVP of the New York Stock Exchange—the original "stock market"—as its CEO.

At its heart StockX is a Detroit story, beginning with the new investment climate Greg has observed. "If you look at our various rounds of financing, we've proven that you can raise a meaningful amount of capital, from all over the world. We have investors like Google Ventures, and Battery Ventures, both renowned traditional Silicon Valley investors. And we're able to do that as a Detroit business! It wasn't because of Detroit per se, but investors appreciated that there are real advantages to the fact that we are headquartered in Detroit." That, obviously, is a new twist to the story—one that is being duplicated all over the country.

TWO

A Shifting Investment Landscape

When I announced that I was starting a venture firm to back entrepreneurial companies, I think most people thought of it as my little side project—more of a hobby than a serious endeavor. The expectation after I stepped down as CEO of AOL was that I'd retire to Hawaii or focus on philanthropy. I wasn't sure what I should do. I was frustrated by the missed opportunities of the merger of AOL and Time Warner, and not all that eager to get back into the "big company" fray. I dabbled with some personal investing for a few years, backing companies like the shared-use car company Zipcar and the vacation club Exclusive Resorts, but after a while an idea moved me—to back the next generation of entrepreneurs, with money but also help, with a bias toward entrepreneurs *outside* of Silicon Valley.

After spending two decades leveling the playing field by driving adoption of the internet, I thought I could potentially have a similar impact in entrepreneurship, for the people and places that had historically been left behind. This was the origin of my investment firm Revolution.

I felt an urgency to succeed. We couldn't afford to have people say, "See, I told you so. You can't really make money investing in startups in the middle of the country. You should just keep doubling down on Silicon Valley, which is where all the winning companies will be." We *had* to be successful to prove that a more expansive, inclusive vision of American innovation was possible. It would not be a trade-off between profit and impact—indeed, the more successful we were as investors, the more likely it was that other investors would follow, and that would multiply the number of entrepreneurs succeeding, and the number of cities rising.

In a sense, funding startups is a bit like running a political campaign. It is well known in politics that early money matters the most, and *credible* early money is the most important of all. Similarly, when entrepreneurs are raising money, people are interested in understanding their story and their company's mission—but the number one question they have is, "Who else has invested?" If a startup doesn't have a credible committed investor, it's often hard to get others to invest. Revolution strives to be that catalytic investor for startups all across the country.

Entrepreneurs need somebody to back them and say, "I'm going to invest in you because I believe in you and believe in your idea." Everything starts with one yes. At Revolution we try to catalyze more yeses. When we go into cities, we lay it on the line with potential local investors who care about the future of their communities, but have often been reluctant to themselves invest in startups. We explain why we think it's the right thing to do, to create jobs and momentum, and also the smart thing to do as investors, because there is more potential in their startup communities than they likely realize. What often happens is that they are inspired to give the entrepreneurs a second look. How can they not?

A CAPITAL REALIGNMENT

Here is my prediction. Over the next decade, a *majority* of the iconic startup companies—the ones that create tens of thousands of jobs and end up being worth billions of dollars—will *not* be in Silicon Valley, but all across the country. It's already happening.

In the last decade, more than a thousand new regional venture firms have started, and they're backing new startups across the country. And while many of these startup communities are in the early stages of development, it's encouraging to see the momentum building.

I've spent much of my career trying to demystify Silicon Valley, even as I've appreciated and celebrated its contribution. Its support network for startups became so fertile that it's no wonder entrepreneurs flocked to the area. And let's cut to the chase—it's been where the money is. For the past decade startups in the state of California, just one of fifty states, have accounted for half of all US venture capital (VC).

Venture capitalists congregated there because that was where most of their fellow venture capitalists resided. It has been easier to raise venture capital if you are located there, and also easier to invest it if you live there. So, Silicon Valley became a magnet for talent, a land of opportunity that has lured innovators from every part of the country and many parts of the world.

I saw this firsthand when I was speaking at a conference in Silicon Valley. More than a thousand people were in the audience, and I asked for a show of hands of how many people grew up in the Bay Area. Just a smattering of the audience raised their hands; it looked to me as if 95 percent were from someplace else.

The landscape started shifting as we entered the Third Wave of the internet. Much of the domain expertise in sectors such as health care, agriculture, transportation, and climate resides in the middle of the country. So do many of the potential business partnerships, suppliers, and support mechanisms. We need Fortune 500 corporations with expertise, credibility, and infrastructure to serve as customers or partners for growing startups, thus creating a business community that innovates with new technologies and talent.

Investors, communities, and local governments are waking up to the fact that most of the job creation in this country does not come from small businesses or big businesses. It comes from new high-growth startups. Therefore, local communities, states, and regions increasingly recognize that it is a worthwhile investment to back startups.

In 2021 Revolution published a study, "Beyond Silicon Valley," with data provided by PitchBook, showing just how dramatic the capital realignment is becoming. Our analysis found that investor interest is increasingly tipping toward "rising cities." Meanwhile, the proportion of early-stage US VC dollars going to Bay Area startups has steadily declined—on pace to see less than 30 percent for the first time in more than a decade. More than $13 billion of Bay Area capital was invested in 2021 outside of the Bay Area, New York, and Boston. A decade earlier that number was $3 billion. Deal volume more than tripled, with more than one thousand rounds in outside ecosystems.

Best of all, new VC firms are launching outside of the major eco-systems. Between 2011 and 2021, 1,445 new venture firms were founded in smaller ecosystems across the country. This is criti-cal, as VC firms in smaller ecosystems are likely to invest more of their dollars in local or regional startups. And their pres-ence in these communities has been a significant accelerator—hometown money creating hometown opportunity.

The network effects so prized in Silicon Valley—the deep density of investor, entrepreneur, and tech talent concentrated in the city with a strong risk-taking appetite—is getting built out in other places. That challenges the investment calculation. Those who have argued for launching startups in Silicon Valley or New York or Boston because it's where the money is can't re-ally make as strong an argument if investors are spreading out to a wider range of cities.

At Rise of the Rest we have found that small but mighty startup communities can help the cities rise, as a more man-ageable, accessible, and founder-friendly market can attract top talent and startups to the region. These cities offer a cost ad-vantage for businesses, based on a lower cost of living and the related lower cost of doing business. With costs skyrocketing in Silicon Valley, New York, and Boston, the attraction of other lo-cations can be meaningful—and sometimes even the difference between life and death for a startup.

THE RISE OF REGIONAL VCS

Those 1,400-plus new venture funds, many focusing on early-stage investments, are seeding a national ecosystem, region by region. Jan Garfinkle is an example of the growing phenomenon of influential regional venture capital firms. Her experience is a road map for both the opportunities and the challenges of trying to raise local money.

After a thriving early career that included working for two medical device startups in Silicon Valley, Jan followed her husband when his job took him to Ann Arbor, Michigan. She had three daughters within eighteen months (a single and twins) and then started a consulting business for local early-stage health care companies. After eight years she decided to make another shift, into venture capital. When she couldn't find a position with an existing firm—there weren't that many—she decided to start her own firm and launched Arboretum Ventures in 2002. Arboretum specializes in backing health care startups.

"I can say from experience that starting a venture capital firm from scratch is never easy and is especially challenging in regions outside traditional VC hubs such as San Francisco or Boston," she told the Senate Subcommittee on Communications, Technology, Innovation, and the Internet during testimony in 2020. "There are a number of structural barriers that exist in under-ventured regions. The lack of investment capital constrains the number of startups that receive funding. Subsequent trickle-down effects include: a reduction in the number of successful exits and secondary reduction of experienced employees who know how to scale a company, which then leads to limited investment capital due to lack of viable investment targets. This downward spiral can be near-insurmountable and requires private and public sector support to overcome."

Jan was a pioneer in regional venture capital, and it took many years for Arboretum to gain traction. Success came with a big show of support from the state of Michigan. The state's Economic Development Corporation recognized that one way to create economic innovation was to stimulate the formation of new venture funds. Arboretum was a beneficiary of that support. Today Arboretum is the largest VC firm in Michigan, with over $700 million under management. It has invested in over fifty companies.

"Build Where You're Strongest" is the motto of Drive Capital, launched in Columbus in 2013 by Chris Olsen and Mark Kvamme. Ohio natives, Chris and Mark were colleagues at Sequoia Capital in Silicon Valley when Mark was recruited by then–Ohio governor John Kasich to work in his administration. One day he was chatting with Chris, and he made a bold declaration: "I think this is the next Silicon Valley. You should start a firm in the Midwest."

"That's the dumbest idea I've ever heard," Chris replied. But when he began to do research, he saw the potential, and he jumped ship in 2012 and headed home. The odds of failure were high, he acknowledged. "But what if we're right?"

Today, with assets under management well in excess of $1 billion, the bet seems to have paid off. But, as history shows, starting a VC firm is hardly a slam dunk, and that's even more true for companies headquartered in the middle of the country.

This isn't the first time people have tried to create regional venture capital firms. There was an earlier wave back in the 1990s. The idea was to raise small VC funds in various cities. The current secretary of commerce, Gina Raimondo, was even part of one of them, a firm called Village Ventures.

In general, the regional VC effort didn't work, for a number of reasons, including a lack of infrastructure to support rapid startup growth in many cities. The traditional people who invest in venture capital firms didn't necessarily buy that there was sufficient deal flow in their regions to necessitate a positive outcome. Even when the states jumped in to help support more investment in local venture funds, they mostly failed to be comparable to coastal funds. The poor experience led to a pullback, and the conclusion, "Regional funds don't work."

That started changing in the last decade as local tech ecosystems began to rise in cities across the country. Suddenly, there were billion-dollar companies coming out of middle American cities, and there was new interest in regional money. After all, who knew these companies better than their own homegrown financiers? What once seemed like a losing bet now showed more promise.

While it's not essential for venture firms to be down the block from the startups they're investing in, there's a special dynamic that occurs when investors are committed to local prosperity and rooting for entrepreneurs to win.

Take KCRise, which is based in Kansas City. Founder and managing director Darcy Howe spent twenty-five years as an angel investor and decided to take a leap into early-stage funding on a deeper level in her hometown. It's likely that entrepreneurs will meet Darcy in person, and that she'll understand what it's like to build a company in their city. More than that, an investment from KCRise will be an important local validator, and KCRise will be an active engaged supporter, through the good times as well as the challenging times.

Here's an example of the difference a local venture fund like KCRise can make. Several years ago, a small group of founders in Kansas City decided to build an online platform for used car auctions, which they named BacklotCars. They received seed capital from KCRise. Because KCRise was connected to other venture firms across the country, including Revolution, when BacklotCars positioned itself to solicit a new round of funding, resources that might once have been earmarked for coastal startups instead found their way to the Midwest. The company was able to use that capital to accelerate its growth, and ultimately exit in what was one of the largest startup acquisitions in Kansas City history.

CREATING CAPITAL MOMENTUM

For a long time one of the most reliable measures of a city's entrepreneurial success was how many unicorns there were. A unicorn is a company valued at over $1 billion. It was named for its statistical rarity, although that's becoming less true. When the term was coined by venture capitalist Aileen Lee, in 2013, there were only thirty-nine unicorns in the United States. As of this writing there are more than one thousand worldwide, more than half of them in the United States. They include well-known companies such as Airbnb, SpaceX, Uber, DraftKings, Stripe, and DoorDash, as well as many that are newer and less well known. In the United States, most unicorns are distinguished by their location in Silicon Valley, but Rise of the Rest cities are beginning to make the cut, with unicorn successes such as Tempus (Chicago), Carvana (Phoenix), Mailchimp (Atlanta), BigCommerce (Austin), and Epic Games (Cary, NC).

There are plenty of lessons to be learned from unicorn companies about the key to their success, but most of them are disrupters in existing industries tackling major felt needs in the community. The Chicago entrepreneur Eric Lefkofsky stands out as an example.

Eric has spent his professional life trying to figure out how to bring technology to industries that don't typically have a lot of technology.

His storied career, which has spanned twenty-five years starting and succeeding at tech companies, began with a moneymaking idea while he was at the University of Michigan. A friend's father owned a carpet store, and Eric suggested they take carpets to school and try to make a little extra "beer and pizza" money selling them. They began selling the carpets, and did very well, turning it into a business. They leaped over every barrier. At one point, early on, the police tried to shut them down because they didn't have a permit, so Eric figured out a way to get a permit. Soon they weren't just selling a dozen carpets from the back of a van; they were selling two to three hundred carpets. Eric received an unexpected bonus from the enterprise. "It was like an aha moment," he said. He realized that he loved being an entrepreneur.

Eric became a classic serial entrepreneur, with an impressive track record of success. His early companies included Innerworkings, which was using technology to automate the inefficiencies of the print business. This segued into the creation of Echo, a logistics and transportation company. Then Eric went on to found MediaOcean, a media buying platform that was sold to Vista. Eric then cofounded Groupon, the social commerce company.

Eric never planned on getting into the health care arena. Then in 2014, his wife was diagnosed with breast cancer. Suddenly, he found himself spending a great deal of time in clinics, talking to a range of doctors and getting differing advice. He was perplexed at how many different therapies were proposed, and he realized how little data was part of his wife's care. At the time, genomic profiling was becoming more readily available for people with cancer, and yet it was very hard to understand how to interpret the results, and how to incorporate them into the care of patients.

Eric is a problem-solver, so he set out to solve that problem by doing what he does best—he started a company, which he named Tempus. The purpose of Tempus was to connect genomic results to clinical data, making diagnostic testing more intelligent. For example, the smart genomic profiling in oncology supports physicians in identifying clinical trials and more targeted, personalized treatment options for their patients.

Eric had spent his career bringing technology to industries that weren't tech-enabled. So, he knew what he was up against, but he also had insights on how to best do it, including forming partnerships with key health care constituencies.

Eric observed that people generally go through a medical scare, such as a cancer diagnosis for themselves or a loved one, in one of two ways. "They retreat and want to put all their faith in their physicians, saying, 'Just tell me what to do and I'll do it. I trust my doctor completely. I don't want to hear about it. I don't want to think about it. Just tell me what to do.' Or they go the other way, which is they really want to understand everything about what's going on with them and they really want to dig deep. I was obviously the latter, and so I became consumed with trying to understand every decision that was being made, why it was being made. So, I just submerged myself pretty deep and out of that came Tempus."

Eric considers himself a proud example that innovation can happen anywhere. "As technology has evolved, and as the internet has become better, as mobile has become better, as videos become better, as the ability to code has become more predominant across the country, it's no longer an art that's mastered by very few people living on the coasts," he said. "You have talented people that are showing up, building amazing businesses all over the world. I think that trend is only going to continue. Right now, we think of technology as a sector, but it's really a background enabler. So, over time, every industry will have a significant technology component, and you're seeing that today with health care."

Tempus (which has also been backed by Revolution Growth) has thrived, developing one of the largest libraries of de-identified clinical and molecular data in cancer and other diseases in the country. It has built the world's largest library of clinical and molecular data and an operating system to make that information accessible and useful for patients, physicians, and researchers.

Eric's advice to aspiring entrepreneurs is clear: "If you tend to be problem-focused and solution-focused, I think those are the most interesting companies that often are more durable than if you're just chasing an outcome, or chasing money, or chasing valuation, or chasing an exit—businesses that over the long horizon tend to be less interesting. So, work on things that are personal to you, or things that you're passionate about, and stay focused on solving problems."

GOVERNMENT PRIORITIZING STARTUPS

For many years, governments focused on small businesses and big businesses, but often neglected startups. That began to change after the 2008 recession when there was significant un- employment, approaching 10 percent. President Obama, who was elected in the throes of the crisis, and Congress, who was sensing growing anxiety from constituents, realized that they had to find a way to create jobs. But how? Some people in government were beginning to recognize that most of the new jobs were being created by young, new, high-growth startups.

In 2010 Congress got onboard, creating the National Advisory Council on Innovation and Entrepreneurship (NACIE) at the Department of Commerce. And Karen Mills, the head of the Small Business Administration (SBA) and a former venture capitalist, began focusing more on high-growth entrepreneurship, as an adjunct to the SBA's more traditional small business focus.

When I was asked to join NACIE, I was skeptical. Government bureaucracies were notable for the slow crawl of progress, and advisory boards often wrote reports that few read or put into action. That said, I saw its potential value and I wanted to be in the room where it was happening. In fact, if I was going to devote time to it, I wanted to help lead the effort. I ended up as one of the cochairs.

We focused on the "three Cs"—capital, community, and celebration. We concluded that there needed to be more of a celebration of entrepreneurship and startups. We realized most entrepreneurs struggled to raise capital, most communities didn't appreciate or support their entrepreneurs, and many cities didn't recognize how pivotal startups were in creating jobs and opportunity.

As an outgrowth of the work of NACIE, President Obama asked me to chair a new White House initiative called Startup America Partnership. The idea was to encourage innovation across the country through the establishment of localized startup hubs in the states. It would be funded jointly by the Case Foundation and the Kauffman Foundation.

We launched the Startup America Partnership with an event

in Cleveland. I flew to Ohio with President Obama on Air Force One. We started our visit at JumpStart, a leader in developing innovative models for economic development. Founder Ray Leach launched JumpStart in 2003 to help northeast Ohio transition from manufacturing to entrepreneurship, so it was the ideal place to kick off our day. Speaking to a group of entrepreneurs, President Obama said, "I did not come to Cleveland to talk. I came here to listen." And what we heard over and over again was that entrepreneurs felt as if they were living on an island, with no place to get advice or support. They were on their own. The magical collaborative spirit that made Silicon Valley great did not exist in their communities. I got it. I remembered struggling with the same isolation when I was building AOL in northern Virginia. I knew that if we were going to encourage innovation, we had to create ecosystems of support, including making investments.

There was another revelation: We needed not only to believe in innovation; we needed to believe in *Cleveland*—or the other cities we were launching in. We wanted to send the message that we were willing to focus on the needs of their communities, realizing that not every community was the same. Our goal was to be a catalyst for a bottom-up movement.

At Startup America Partnership I encouraged people to ask themselves, "What is your part in the tapestry of entrepreneurship?" We were attracting many young people with a passion for making a difference who were motivated by the grassroots nature of our program. This ultimately became a model for Rise of the Rest.

As the internet becomes more integrated into our daily lives, and as more of our processes become tech-enabled, it stands to reason that the big problems we face, such as climate change,

food insecurity, and inequality, can be tackled by creative entrepreneurs. In the health arena alone, countless startups are
working toward breakthroughs that will increase longevity and
cure disease. On the road with Rise of the Rest it is becoming
increasingly common to hear entrepreneurs express a desire to
change the world, or at least their corner of the world. It's not
enough to do something cool; they want to do something that
matters.

THREE

How to Build a Tech Ecosystem

In 2013, Salesforce, a huge cloud-based software company in San Francisco, acquired ExactTarget, a homegrown Indianapolis marketing software and services company, for $2.5 billion. In a decision that surprised many, Salesforce chose to leave the company in Indianapolis. It bought the tallest building in the city, which fronted the major circle in the middle of downtown, refurbished it, and rebranded it Salesforce Tower. (The original Salesforce Tower in San Francisco is also the tallest building in that city.) The commitment to Indianapolis made all the difference.

Momentum begets momentum, and ExactTarget's founders, Scott Dorsey, Chris Baggott, and Peter McCormick, were instrumental in creating a flywheel that led to a stronger startup ecosystem. It's a powerful example of what happens when you have a success story that is driven by founders who then reinvest in the ecosystem. And these successful tech ecosystems really do lift all boats, not just in tech but also in supporting industries. Indy's broader community benefited from the fresh vitality and the demand for services generated by ExactTarget.

In October 2017, Rise of the Rest came to town on the red bus, to see the Indy startup community for ourselves. We visited a variety of coworking spaces designed to create network density. This included Developer Town, a massive hangar where innovators take small, prefabricated houses and design them for their teams. Other teams are just "next door," allowing for collaboration. We also visited High Alpha, a venture studio that invests in and incubates new ideas, founded by Scott Dorsey, the ExactTarget cofounder.

We joined founders and civic leaders, including then-senator Joe Donnelly, for lunch at the Indy Motor Speedway. The setting had a lot of symbolism, connecting the old and the new. We encouraged these policymakers to support entrepreneurship locally and across the state. Also joining us was Indianapolis-born Ron Klain, a cofounder of Revolution, who played a pivotal role in the launch of Rise of the Rest before he went on to serve the country as President Biden's chief of staff.

We ended the day at Union 525, a tech incubator housed in a century-old former high school building in the downtown area. There we met with leadership and students from Purdue Polytechnic, a magnet school supported by Purdue and focused on STEM. This charter school was founded after Purdue University president Mitch Daniels discovered that fewer than ten of Purdue's engineering students came from the Indianapolis public school system. Purdue Polytechnic was created to fill that gap. In its first year it had 130 students from around Indianapolis.

The finale, as always, was the pitch competition, which was being held in the restored gymnasium, where a sold-out crowd was packed in, noisy and excited. The ten finalists (from one hundred entrants) vying for the $100,000 investment ranged from Go Electric, an energy solutions company; to Torchlight, which connects marketers to experts to manage campaigns; to 120Water, an at-home water testing kit.

When Megan Glover, the founder of 120Water, gave her four-minute pitch, I was immediately intrigued. The idea was simple to grasp, completely original, and it addressed a true need in the community. She'd only been at it a year, but it was the kind of project that could scale. From the start I felt there was a bigger idea, a broader application than a consumer product, that could be groundbreaking for communities.

As I listened to the ten pitches, I found all of them compelling, but I kept coming back to 120Water. What struck me about Megan's startup was that it was addressing a major societal problem. She'd been inspired by the water crisis in nearby Flint—so the stakes were much higher. Months before she made her pitch, she'd received a contract from the city of Pittsburgh to test the water in its schools, which was a big breakthrough. None of the other pitch ideas matched the impact potential of Megan's company. Megan won the competition.

Before launching her startup, Megan had been part of the startup community in Indianapolis for years. She'd been a marketing executive at many companies, including Angie's List. "I fell in love with the business at Angie's List," she said. "It's where I really realized I wanted to be in marketing and on the front end of businesses. What I ended up doing for Angie's is building their first ever digital marketing strategy, which was very cool. So, from there, I knew that I wanted an executive level path as a CMO or in marketing for an entrepreneurial type company. I also fell in love with the burgeoning Indianapolis tech community while I was at Angie's List."

One day she was having coffee with ExactTarget cofounder

Chris Baggott, who had become a mentor. They were there to talk about Chris's new startup, but the conversation drifted to the situation in Flint.

When Megan had first read about the Flint, Michigan, water crisis in 2016, she'd felt a chilling sense of horror and a nagging fear. She lived in Zionsville, a small suburb northwest of Indianapolis, and although she was three hundred miles from Flint, she identified with the crisis there. If it could happen in Flint, it could happen anywhere. As a mother of two, Megan was very serious about what her family ate and drank. But this was the first time she'd given serious thought to the safety of the water supply.

"Have you ever thought about testing your water?" Chris asked Megan. She hadn't, but the question stayed with her. In this day and age, when she could buy hormone-free milk and organic snacks for her kids, why did she have to worry about her water? She wondered if there was a way to find out if their drinking water was safe and decided to find out.

She contacted her local water utility. "I'd like to get my water tested," she said. The reply was, "We don't do that. That's not a service that we provide. You can call a lab." She called a lab and was told, "We don't do one-off sampling requests." They recommended a water testing company that would charge her $3,000 to conduct a test. Megan was appalled. There must be a better way for people to test their water and make sure it's safe.

Megan went back to Chris and said, "I don't know what's here. This idea isn't fully baked, but I just went to try and test my water and I couldn't. I think we should go further with this idea." Chris agreed, and along with another partner they raised around $135,000 and within about eight weeks started the company.

It was a long shot, but she believed in the cause. "Water found me," she explained.

In the coming months Megan devised a plan and came up with a name, 120Water, the number referring to the frequency at which consumers should test their water (every 120 days). Her idea was for an inexpensive and simple product—basically a box containing a beaker for the water sample and a prepaid envelope to send it to an EPA-certified lab. Results would be returned via email. The kit would cost between $54 and $84, depending on the type of analysis.

The barriers were high. Megan was not from the industry, nor was she a chemical or environmental engineer. For a year she worked out of her parents' garage to ship kits.

Through it all, the startup community in Indianapolis was a big factor in her success. "It takes a village," she said. And she found it mattered even more when her business expanded to selling to government agencies and municipalities. "We decided we were going to raise our first round of funding and could not have done it without the support of the community in Indianapolis. I remember Chris's mother saying, 'This is an idea that deserves a runway.' There are a lot of ideas on the coast that get funded, just by writing two sentences on the back of a napkin. It's more difficult to raise funds here in Indiana. But I had my peers and the people who believed in 120 and who made sure that the right people got a look at it, and they helped us succeed."

Megan's Rise of the Rest win catalyzed the remarkable growth of her company, which now includes cloud-based software in executing testing and compliance programs for government agencies, schools, and others. In September 2019, 120Water announced $7 million in Series A funding, which allowed her to hire more than one hundred people, putting the company well on its way to national expansion.

As Megan staffs her company, she's reaching out to what she calls the "boomerang Hoosiers"—those who have left Indiana to go to Apple or Twitter and are now interested in coming back. It's a pitch with a lot of appeal—all the excitement of tech innovation, plus the breathing room, affordability, and family connections of Indiana—as well as the chance to do something meaningful for the world from your own backyard.

"I think it's very rare professionally to get up and do what you love every day and build something that has a big impact on the world," Megan said. "Our solution has been deployed in the US to impact over 15 million lives. And my chest gets a little heavy just because, up until this point, I've never been in a position where I'm building or selling something that actually has a direct impact on public health. And my kids know exactly what we do, and they've learned all about water. They've learned about why it's so important, and the things they need to be thinking about to build more resilient water communities in the future. It's so rewarding to get out every day and share this experience with my kids because what we're doing matters, not just for our generation but for generations to come."

THE ECOSYSTEM WHEEL

I tell Megan's story to illustrate the dynamic interconnectedness of the tech ecosystem. Even when entrepreneurs have the best ideas in the world, they have trouble getting out of the gate without a network behind them. The Indy dynamic, with Exact-Target as a tentpole—a company around which others are built and thrive—has created greater local opportunity for aspiring entrepreneurs.

Think of the tech ecosystem as a wheel with seven spokes, connected and in motion. The spokes are comprised of: (1) start-ups, (2) investors, (3) universities, (4) government, (5) corporations, (6) startup support organizations, and (7) local media. These entities use a variety of levers to help convene, educate, inform, and link startups. Their efforts, in turn, inspire an environment that is conducive to innovation and entrepreneurship.

The defining characteristic of the ecosystem wheel is the collective activity of this ecosystem support network. It's important to underscore that these entities don't operate independently of one another. This isn't a list; it's a wheel. The impact of one is in relationship to the impact of the others. And while a young startup might not have all the spokes in motion, that usually happens with successful companies.

We saw an example of the wheel in motion with our Indianapolis tentpole, ExactTarget. We're always on the lookout for tentpoles, and we find them in every corner of the nation. Often their elevation comes through an integration with a large existing company, which is what happened with Shipt, a Birmingham, Alabama, grocery delivery service, which was acquired by Target for $550 million. Remaining in Birmingham, Shipt provided a significant boost to the local economy with a plan to hire nearly one thousand workers. The same thing happened in Michigan. When Cisco acquired Duo Security, an Ann Arbor cybersecurity company, in 2018, for $2.4 billion, it became the largest acquisition in the state of Michigan. Duo Security's cofounder and CEO Dug Song had made the transaction contingent on the company remaining in Michigan. Song believed that the company's success was intimately tied to its location, and he'd made it his mission to support the next generation of entrepreneurs in Ann Arbor.

Often, legacy corporations make the difference in vaulting startups to another level. Increasingly, these companies are taking their role of helping to build startup ecosystems seriously. We've seen this in Atlanta, where AT&T, Delta, Home Depot, and Southern Company have opened more than fifteen innovation centers in Georgia Tech's Tech Square. We've also seen it in places where particular industries dominate. For example, the concentration of finance and insurance companies in Des Moines, which is home to the headquarters of Allied Insurance and the Principal Financial Group Inc. and is a significant location for Wells Fargo Home Mortgage, has turned Des Moines into a center of finance and insurance-related jobs. Several local insurance companies pooled resources there to form the nation's first insurance technology—or "insurtech"—accelerator.

Existing companies, local governments, and investors are instrumental in keeping the ecosystem wheel in motion through the development of different kinds of startup support organizations. These are the visible networking activities that bring startup communities together, support them, and educate the next generation of innovators. In various cities you'll find incubators, which are physical spaces for startup development with support staff and equipment. You'll find accelerators, which, as the name suggests, help startups grow, with a full range of programs, tools, mentorship, education, and financing. You'll find community builders—those individuals who commit to a larger purpose and bring others together. As we saw in the last chapter, these startup support organizations also help connect young businesses to the investment community.

The underpinning of tech ecosystems often involves government partnerships that back startup communities both financially and institutionally, considering them a big bet on the future. Charleston is a signature example of the way government incentives can help boost startup innovation and development. Designed to attract and retain area entrepreneurs and their growing companies, the Charleston suburb of Mount Pleasant offers the Economic Development Incentive Grant program, a homegrown investment program that offers investments in companies that add to the tax base, create clean, high-paying jobs, and are compatible with the environment. In Arkansas, the Equity Investment Incentive Program offers an income tax credit to investors purchasing equity investments in some new technology-based businesses. Other states have similar efforts, to stimulate more VC investment and support more startups. On every Rise of the Rest tour, we've had public officials present who serve as hands-on partners, and often leaders of these innovation efforts.

We've also found that one of the most consistent driving forces in the emergence of successful ecosystems is universities, which are often the leading laboratories for innovation.

We find a strong example in Durham at Duke University, with the Innovation & Entrepreneurship Initiative, which forms a hub for entrepreneurs that pulls together resources from other schools and departments. The Initiative was so successful that two years after it was established it moved off the Duke campus to a downtown location that is soon to be the site of the planned Duke Innovation District. Johns Hopkins of Baltimore is another example of university impact. In particular, its FastForward program offers phenomenal support for startups, with access to 40,000 square feet of office, coworking, and lab space; equipment; experienced mentors; legal and accounting services; and opportunities to network with investors.

I've included local media in the ecosystem wheel because it is often the key to amplifying startup news. Examples include local hybrids such as Dallas Innovates and Refresh Miami, which provide a mix of news, data, and thought leadership for the tech community; and GeekWire, a Seattle tech news site that has gained a large and loyal audience.

Very often there is a lack of awareness or understanding of what is happening with startups in a city. So much coverage and attention has been given over the years to legacy companies that even people in the business community are unaware of the exciting startup movements in their own backyard. Local press can help overcome that barrier and bring new local attention, investment, and partnerships to burgeoning startups. It can also lead to national coverage and attention.

The "seven spokes" is not a magic formula. Startups don't have to check every box in order to thrive. I've heard entrepreneurs express discouragement because they didn't live in an area with a top research university. I tell them we see cities where entrepreneurs have done well without that. However, the ecosystem wheel is predictive of which cities will rise the fastest.

A FOUNDER FINDS ECCSYSTEM PARTNERS

Lindsay Tjepkema is another example of the tech vitality that has been created in Indianapolis. As a brand management expert, Lindsay was always asking how to make brands as human as possible. That is, how to build relationships and create trust.

To her frustration, she found that the B2B marketing teams she encountered were often operating from an outdated playbook.

When she began to think of creating a new platform, she turned to the Indianapolis tech ecosystem—specifically, the High Alpha Venture Studio. High Alpha is a cutting-edge approach to ecosystem development, serving as a company builder, not just a funder.

High Alpha's cofounder and managing partner Scott Dorsey reached out to Lindsay and they talked about the opportunity. "There's a reckoning coming in B2B marketing and content marketing as a whole," she told him, describing how the technologies and the channels were changing, but the playbook was remaining the same. She described her idea for the startup that would become Casted, a video podcast platform created for B2B marketers.

"Scott said, 'Let's do this thing together,'" Lindsay recalled, and just like that she had the support and know-how of Alpha Studio—a pretty big buffer for someone who knew next to nothing about creating a startup.

The decision to leave her job and embark on a startup felt natural to Lindsay, even though by some metrics it was a crazy choice. "I had three little boys at home and a husband with an equally demanding job," she said. "Am I going to leave a secure company to start something new? Of course I am!"

The reason, she said, was that she couldn't imagine not doing it. "The idea that somebody else could possibly come along and do this instead of me absolutely crushed me. And if someone asks, 'Why me?' I say, 'Why not me?' This business is the culmination of my entire career and every single observation, win, loss, frustration, great idea, bad idea that I've experienced for twenty years."

Revolution Ventures recognized Casted's potential in 2019, leading the Series A funding. And that was *before* the pandemic. When COVID hit, all the humanizing effects of Lindsay's platform were in desperate demand, and Casted's revenue and customer base skyrocketed during 2020. They started 2020 with ten employees and closed the year with forty-two and climbing, with a plan to become a hybrid company.

For Lindsay, the core values of the business remain the same. "People are wired for connection," she said. "And because business is human, regardless of what you're selling, we are humans selling to other humans. The more human a business is, the more people will trust it." That's the understanding she was passionate about infusing in her business model.

LOUISVILLE: An Ecosystem Built on Love

On a warm May afternoon in 2018, the Rise of the Rest team was enjoying a break at Porkland Barbecue in the Portland neighborhood of Louisville, Kentucky. As we ate pulled pork sandwiches, rib tips, sausage, and tater tots slathered in special sauce, one of our team remarked, "This, to me, is entrepreneurship." He wasn't wrong.

Porkland Barbecue is part of a unique community development experiment in one of Louisville's poorest neighborhoods. The founders, Shawn and Inga Arvin, have named the project Love City, as a nod to their Christian values and also to the community spirit they promote of lifting each other up.

In the midst of a busy day visiting startups and meeting with local Louisville businesses, Love City might have been just one in a line of stops. But every so often an organization or group of people has the potential to reach out and touch us in a special way. Years after that day, our team still points to Love City when they talk about a community that made a lasting impression.

Love City also teaches us that innovation is not just a flashy tech word. True innovation means transforming communities. In the case of Love City, tech and community come together to enrich people's lives and build a future.

When Shawn Arvin started talking, the room was still. During the tour we had heard many startup pitches from remarkable entrepreneurs that excited and inspired us. Shawn's story of community, possibility, and love was so moving it left everyone in tears. It was the most impressive and captivating pitch that we heard all day.

Shawn described how he and Inga launched a bold new life in 2014—moving from the upscale Louisville neighborhood of Crescent Hill to Portland, one of the poorest. Simply put, Portland called to them. Shawn had grown up nearby with a struggling single mother, and through grit and determination had transcended his roots, graduating from college, pursuing a career, and marrying Inga, whom he met in Rome where they were both part of Bellarmine University's executive MBA program. The way Shawn tells it, one day Inga simply said that they should move to Portland and be part of helping a struggling community, and he agreed.

Initially, they planned only to live there. But when they bought a house, they were told it came with a boarded-up building next door that had once been a community center. Inspired by the idea of making a difference, they restored the center and started their nonprofit, Love City. They have a simple principle: community comes first. In order to achieve and progress, the community must be strong.

By the time we came through in 2018, the Love City community center was a thriving operation, with clubs, classes, tutoring, summer camps, and open gym time. It was championed by local entrepreneurs and government leaders. Google Fiber, Alphabet's high-speed internet provider, built a startup incubator in the community center. There was internet access through Google, smart speakers, tablets and screens, and a physical upgrade to make it a comfortable space in which to do business. It opened with great fanfare in a community celebration.

At a nearby location, on the campus of the former St. Cecilia Church, the community opened Porkland, where we enjoyed our lunch. An interesting note about the restaurant, which is the only sit-down restaurant in the neighborhood: it has a "pay what you can" policy. Porkland also accepts help in the restaurant in exchange for food, and all the tips received are put toward meals for people who are unable to pay.

This was my second visit to Louisville. I'd been there in June 2016 for a quick one-day event, which was organized as part of my *Third Wave* book tour. Chuck Denny, then the regional president of PNC Bank and a local force of nature, had been instrumental in getting me there. Once I was on the ground, Chuck proceeded to give me a tour with a lot of impact. Chuck's love for his hometown was evident everywhere we went, and at the end of the day he was eager to hear what I thought. I was honest. There were many startups with great promise, but I told Chuck that the scene was too scattered. "It doesn't feel like there's a center of gravity," I told him. "Maybe you should look at building something physical that can serve as a gathering place and a connector."

Chuck took my words to heart. He was determined, and he spent the next two years plotting a way to get his beloved Louisville on the Rise of the Rest bus tour schedule. In 2018, when we did a "Bring Back the Bus" campaign, we invited all the places we'd visited to compete for our return. Louisville beat out the other cities—it wasn't even close! Chuck mobilized the university, he got the mayor involved, and they made a concerted effort. So, the Rise of the Rest bus returned.

When we arrived and I greeted Chuck, the size of his smile could light up a room. On that visit he was proud to show me the "central place" I'd suggested they create—the gleaming 1804 Entrepreneurship Center, named for the year Lewis and Clark set out from Louisville on their famous expedition. It was showing early signs of becoming a thriving gathering place to connect and empower the startup ecosystem.

Early in the day, we hosted an outdoor breakfast where then-governor Matt Bevin and Louisville mayor Greg Fischer spoke of their commitment to supporting Louisville's startup culture. Fischer was a critical advocate for entrepreneurs, not just in Kentucky but throughout the country, and he invited me to address the US Conference of Mayors when it met in Louisville. These strong alliances with local, state, and federal government leaders are essential for the growth of rising startup communities. While the entrepreneurs themselves are at the center, starting and scaling companies, the context in which they operate is largely established by public officials, who are elected by the people.

Louisville prides itself on its entrepreneurial history. For example, Humana, the health care provider and Fortune 500 company, started there. David Jones, the then-eighty-five-year-old Humana founder and its CEO for four decades, was in the audience for our Rise of the Rest lunch in Louisville. He was a giant in Louisville, not just for his extraordinary business success but because of all he had done to lift up the community. His presence was a huge signal to the rest of the attendees that this was an important moment for Louisville entrepreneurs—all the more because he had some health struggles, but still made it to the lunch. (Sadly, he passed away two years later.)

"When Humana started everybody thought it was a crazy idea," I said when we gathered at the Entrepreneurial Center. "Most thought health care was too hard to change—and if it *did* change, it was hard to imagine a little startup from Kentucky would be the change agent. Few believed in David, or Humana, or the entrepreneurs in Louisville. But he fought on, and prevailed, building a $50 billion company, right here. And now he's joining with us to help the next generation of entrepreneurs do it again."

Louisville was on the lookout for the *next* Humana. The goal was to build on the strengths of the city, including its leadership in sectors like health care, and create a more fertile environment for startups.

I suggested to the audience that Louisville could benefit by thinking of itself as part of a broader region that also includes nearby Midwestern cities, such as Cincinnati, Indianapolis, and Nashville. They could draw resources from each other and help each other grow. That's an example of what we mean when we talk about entrepreneurship as a team sport.

I remember on the early tours that we talked a lot about who we were doing this for. Were we doing it for the delegation—those investors and corporate dignitaries coming along on the bus—or were we doing it for the local community? I decided it was both. We're bringing the corporate leaders out of their headquarters and really engaging them with startups in a way most couldn't have experienced otherwise. At the same time, we're exposing, celebrating, engaging—and hopefully *inspiring*—the local community.

But there's another big piece of this with the people that we invite to come on tour with us, and that's the homecoming factor. Once the word got out that we were going to be traveling to all these local communities in every part of the country, there was a groundswell of interest from successful entrepreneurs who wanted to come on the bus with us. Many of these entrepreneurs remembered a time when they were coming up and had to leave their hometowns to go to New York or Silicon Valley to build their companies—because that's what people did to be successful. But now they saw that we were bringing some of the top investors in the country into their hometowns!

Then-PayPal COO Bill Ready (now president of commerce at Google) was one of those people to join the Louisville tour. Bill grew up in rural Kentucky and had few advantages. He didn't even know how to use a computer until he got to college. But he had big dreams. Bill sat down with me for a fireside chat at the University of Louisville at the end of the day. He encouraged the aspiring entrepreneurs, reminding them that Silicon Valley doesn't have a monopoly on innovation and problem-solving. "Don't be afraid to get into the game," he said. "If you see a problem that needs to be solved, it's easier than ever to get into it. And now, more than ever, you can do it from right here."

One of my favorite stops in downtown Louisville was the Muhammad Ali Center. Motto: "Be great . . . do great things." Ali was born and raised in Louisville, and became a wonderful, positive role model for courage and conviction, and achieving against the odds. He spent most of his life learning to get back up when he was knocked down, but perhaps his greatest challenge was Parkinson's disease, which he never let stop him. In every interview in his final years, he was glowing and inspirational.

The six core principles of the Muhammad Ali Center easily apply to everyone who wants to make a difference in the world, including entrepreneurs:

Confidence: Belief in oneself, one's abilities, and one's future.
Conviction: A firm belief that gives one the courage to stand behind that belief, despite pressure to do otherwise.
Dedication: The act of devoting all of one's energy, effort, and abilities to a certain task.
Giving: To present voluntarily without expecting something in return.
Respect: Esteem for, or a sense of the worth or excellence of, oneself and others.
Spirituality: A sense of awe, reverence, and inner peace inspired by a connection to all of creation and/or that which is greater than oneself.

As we toured the center, I took note of a famous Ali saying, as it was especially relevant to entrepreneurs: "It isn't the mountains ahead to climb that wear you out; it's the pebble in your shoe."

MADISON: The Startup Roundtable

Madison, Wisconsin, has many advantages as a tech ecosystem. Quintessentially Midwest in terms of values and work ethic, and endowed with a fabulous university, it has leaned into the idea of creating the next generation of startup leaders. Some of the energy is propelled by the university, but much of it is also driven by local entrepreneurs.

On a trip through Wisconsin during one of our annual RV vacation trips, my wife, Jean, and I stopped in Madison to have dinner with Scott Cook, the founder of Intuit, and his wife, Signe, who grew up in Madison. They invited some of their friends, many of whom had worked at the Oscar Mayer Company during high school and in their careers. When Oscar Mayer shut down the Madison plant in 2016 as part of a restructuring effort, one thousand people were laid off. It was a tremendous economic blow to the area, one of many once-thriving businesses that shuttered.

The only way out of the decline was to find ways to create more jobs, and that's where startups come in. A strong collaboration between the University of Wisconsin–Madison, the Wisconsin Alumni Research Foundation (WARF), and University Research Park has created an emerging ecosystem for startups that includes a WARF accelerator, an entrepreneurial mentorship program named MERLIN Mentors, a campus coworking and innovation hub called @1403, and an early-stage support program to help entrepreneurs get to market.

Scott Resnick is a Madison evangelist—a personable, high-spirited young man who has devoted himself to reinventing Madison as a tech center. Scott, a graduate of the University of Wisconsin–Madison, was elected to the Common Council within two years of graduation and became a driving force of ecosystem development in the city.

Even though Scott was only twenty-three years old when he became a public official, he knew what he wanted to contribute to the city, and often made speeches touting Madison as the future center of innovation. He continually asked, "How can we modernize government? How can we modernize our community and our economy to ensure upward mobility?"

It was a pressing question for the times because it was the end of an industrial era in Madison. "It was an inflection point," Scott said. "There was no answer as to how Madison was going to turn around. It seemed as if there were two options: the community could reach for new challenges, or it could wither—as many college towns had. So, we doubled down on creating success in the startup community."

Before, there was a smattering of biotech and other deals that didn't add up to a strong, tech-focused ecosystem. But that picture has changed. Today, Scott noted, LinkedIn calls Madison one of the hottest growth locations for technical development in the country, and dozens of startups are having success.

It was a steep climb to get there. When Scott and his friends from college came out of school and got started, they realized there was no landscape for entrepreneurship. "We were right out of the university and were out in the real world. It is a cold, dark place. You didn't know who you could talk to about venture capital. You didn't know which lawyers understood how to help you scale your company. You didn't know which accountants you could trust because there weren't that many of them. So, we ended up creating what essentially became a roundtable group, called Capital Entrepreneurs, and we met once a month. We had seven members and it was just a few founders, including myself, talking about how hard it is to be an entrepreneur." But they were on to something. The group kept growing, until it had reached three hundred members, becoming an active community.

In 2012, Capital Entrepreneurs proposed a novel idea: What if they bought a building together and moved their startups in and created a nonprofit? Then, instead of having to pay land-lords, they could put the money back into the startup commu-nity. That was the origin of StartingBlock, which was a physical manifestation of Scott's dream of making Madison an innova-tion center.

"We didn't know what we were doing," he admitted. "We were all in our early to mid-twenties. I was serving on the plan-ning commission, but I knew nothing about real estate devel-opment. I knew just enough to be dangerous when I walked into a room. I'd never applied for a loan before. And this was big. But we were able to form public-private partnerships, and six years later we were able to create a 50,000-square-foot facil-ity and raise $10 million—part of a larger $80 million public-private, mixed-use development to basically build the home of entrepreneurship in Madison." In the beginning, the most common word they heard was "No," but gradually they enlisted some corporate players, such as American Family Insurance. The City of Madison, the local gas and utility, and the Univer-sity of Wisconsin–Madison also became partners. They broke ground in January 2017, with Scott tapped to serve as Starting-Block's first executive director.

Others have stepped up to support Madison's entrepre-neurial community. Notably, Chamber of Commerce president Zach Brandon has made startups a priority for the chamber. His Madison Pressure Chamber events have become a pitch com-petition staple of the community. Winners receive the "golden suitcase," an invitation to join the chamber at startup meetings with Silicon Valley investment firms.

The landscape in Madison has changed a great deal since Scott and his fellow entrepreneurs articulated their vision. "When we started this process, there was no nomenclature for even being an ecosystem, let alone an entrepreneur," Scott said. "Today, you can almost choose anywhere in the world to live, and still be a functional member of a company. If communities are going to thrive, they have to provide quality of life, be places where people want to live—whether that's a clean, strong environment, good schools, parks and bike paths, or a vibrant downtown."

Scott is an example of the generational promise that exists for these emerging tech communities. Looking back on his upbringing, he notes the limits to potential—his mom was an administrative assistant, and his dad was a disk jockey. They had a loving family life, but at the time, people were pretty much siloed in their careers, with few options. Now, when he looks at his family, which includes a wife and two small children, he realizes that it's very different. "It comes down to social mobility, the American dream," he said. "That's so much of what entrepreneurship is about—the opportunity to build something bigger than yourself. And the Rise of the Rest vision is coming into being—you can do it anywhere."

FOUR

Stronger Together

We know that ecosystem success depends on entrepreneurs being in close, regular contact with other creators who share the passion, skills, and tools for building a startup community. No matter where you live, there are benefits to clustering people and services together. That way, the collaboration that fuels creativity, which is especially important in the early days of a startup, can be intensified. And the serendipity of finding allies for your cause—one of the untold secrets of successful startups—can be maximized.

There are different ways of achieving this effect, called network density. Many cities are setting up physical spaces for entrepreneurs to work, share ideas, and solve problems. In turn, these gathering places have served as engines of transformation, helping to revitalize often-neglected city centers.

GREEN BAY: Titletown Tech

When the fans own the team—especially when it is an iconic team like the Green Bay Packers—magic can happen. And I'm not just talking about on the field. The Packers are helping lead the charge in transforming Green Bay into a thriving innovation hub. Green Bay was quite aggressive in pitching a Rise of the Rest visit, and what a story they had to tell.

This is another case of a small city—population around 105,000—that is pursuing the development of a tech community. It all happened as an ingenious collaboration between a local business leader named Craig Dickman, owner of Breakthrough Fuel, who had a vision of what Green Bay could become, the Green Bay Packers, and Microsoft.

When Craig launched Breakthrough Fuel in 2004 to help companies cut shipping costs, he got resistance—even from potential customers. They'd tell him, "This looks like an innovative idea, but you're in Green Bay, Wisconsin. Can it really be that good?" People regularly told him he should move to the coast to attract top talent and establish market cred. He staunchly refused. "This is where I grew up," he explained. "I went to high school here, went to college here. My mom still lives in the house I grew up in, at eighty-seven years old. I wanted to build here. And I think there is a certain stubbornness that comes from being tied to community that says, 'There's no reason we can't build here.'"

His bet worked. Breakthrough Fuel ended up attracting people from all over the country, including the coasts, because they wanted to work on meaningful problems. As a result, he built a global business in Green Bay. In the process he also got together with a core group of owners to found the N.E.W. (Northeast Wisconsin) Venture Foundry as a network for startups. It laid the groundwork for future efforts.

It certainly paid off in the following years as Craig, having sold his company, entered a new arena that would have tremendous implications for Green Bay's startup community.

The engine that fueled the change was the Green Bay Packers. Around the time Craig was selling Breakthrough Fuel he was approached about the Packers' interest in doing something big for the community. Packers president Mark Murphy was particularly interested in how they could advance entrepreneurship and innovation, giving talent a reason to come and grow and stay in Green Bay. "They wanted to know, 'How can we be part of building an ecosystem?'" Craig said. Craig got involved—he was the experienced entrepreneur in the room—and they began to talk about what kind of ecosystem they could build with the Packers' resources. "We recognized that capital was going to be part of it," Craig acknowledged, "but the heart was going to be this capability to work side by side with founders and entrepreneurs to really build and really create, and that became our focus."

By chance, while they were working on this idea, a *Milwaukee Journal Sentinel* reporter introduced Mark Murphy to Microsoft president Brad Smith. Smith happened to be a native of Appleton, Wisconsin, a half hour away from Green Bay, and he had a personal love for the community. Murphy began telling him about the plan they were working on, and Smith mentioned that Microsoft had an interest in moving some of its philanthropy and community activities to other regions. Both men thought there might be something there. They brought Craig into the conversation, and they began the process of figuring out whether they could form a partnership that met their and the community's needs.

The result was TitletownTech, named for Green Bay's proud moniker. Using a forty-five-acre empty plot of land next to Lambeau Field where the Packers play, a TitletownTech Center would be built to contain an innovation lab, a venture studio, and the commitment of a venture fund to help build and scale companies. Craig was tapped to be one of two general managers. The other was Jill Enos, an entrepreneur who had been instrumental in creating the N.E.W. Venture Foundry.

It seemed like fate when the launch of TitletownTech was officially announced by the Packers and Microsoft in October 2017, at the same time the Rise of the Rest bus was arriving in town, but Craig had probably planned it all along. He'd spearheaded a social media campaign to bring us to Green Bay, promoting it as #ThePlaceForCase. That caught our attention, and when we learned about TitletownTech and the other initiatives, we were eager to include Green Bay on our tour. This small community was achieving its own version of tech network density.

The 46,000-square-foot TitletownTech Center was completed in 2019. I returned in late 2021 to see the finished product, and along with my wife, Jean (who had chosen to celebrate her birthday by attending a Packers game at Lambeau Field), met with Craig, Jill, and more than a dozen entrepreneurs who were part of TitletownTech.

The building is split into three levels: level one is home to community engagement and public-use space that allows members of the community to engage with the technology entrepreneurs and innovators in the region. Levels two and three are home to TitletownTech's three programming arms: the Innovation Lab, the Venture Studio, and the $25 million Venture

Fund. The N.E.W. Venture Foundry serves as an incubator, and there is enthusiastic involvement by the University of Wisconsin system and the University of Wisconsin–Green Bay.

Love of Green Bay spurs them on. Craig is happy to discuss the benefits of doing business there—not just the relatively low cost of living and appealing quality of life but a great team spirit, off the field as well as on. A strong sense of ownership pervades every endeavor. Now, with TitletownTech, Green Bay will have an anchor for an innovation hub.

"We don't want to be the next Silicon Valley," Craig told us. "We want to be unique in solving problems that we're well positioned to solve, some of the most meaningful problems in the market. And we can do it here in the upper Midwest."

PHOENIX: Innovation District

When Rise of the Rest first visited Phoenix in 2016, we found a city that was coming into its own as a startup arena, with the encouragement of two powerful patrons—Arizona State University (ASU) under the leadership of its president Michael Crow, and the City of Phoenix under the leadership of Mayor Greg Stanton. I had worked with Michael when we both served on the National Advisory Council on Innovation and Entrepreneurship, and I found him to be a brilliant strategist and systems thinker. Michael has transformed ASU into one of the most innovative universities in the country, and he then used ASU's significant footprint in Phoenix to transform the city itself.

Greg Stanton began his mayoral term in 2012 during a time when the city was still struggling to emerge from the recession.

Startup activity was sporadic and lacked a unifying center. Among other initiatives, Greg set his sights on a depressed area south of downtown known as the Warehouse District. In the late nineteenth and early twentieth centuries, this was a thriving center of warehousing and product movement, with horse-drawn vehicles crowding the streets, crisscrossed with railroad spurs for loading and unloading train cars. Vast quantities of agricultural product were loaded onto boxcars, refrigerated by ice blocks, and distributed throughout the area. But by the mid-twentieth century, the vital shipping and production hub had gone silent, the buildings falling into disrepair. Many of them remained standing, corroding from within for lack of use.

By the turn of the twenty-first century the Warehouse District was a wasteland—Greg called it a desert—largely abandoned by city government and business. When Greg took office, he set his sights on turning the decline around with an ambitious plan to transform the Warehouse District into a center of technology, innovation, art, and culture. To accomplish this, he needed a range of partners that brought together local strengths and a sense of identity—such as the rich immigrant history.

The Warehouse District project was in the early developmental stage when Rise of the Rest visited in 2016, but the ecosystem was beginning to come together. By 2019, the project was thriving. It still had enthusiastic support from Arizona State University and the City of Phoenix, and Mayor Stanton continued as a champion after he moved on to serve in Congress. Corporate support came from Marriott and the Phoenix Suns and Arizona Diamondbacks sports teams.

The most successful emerging ecosystems recognize that scaling a startup requires network density—being in close, regular contact with other creators who share a willingness to explore what is possible.

CINCINNATI: Over-the-Rhine's Union Hall

Over-the-Rhine used to be known as one of America's most dangerous neighborhoods—and that was not much more than a decade ago. North of downtown Cincinnati, the once-thriving German working-class community (thus the name) saw collapse in the final decades of the twentieth century as industrial jobs disappeared. Yet, in 2014 we were attracted to Cincinnati and the emerging ecosystem that was revitalizing Over-the-Rhine and other neighborhoods.

The key was the dedication of leaders who refused to accept the decline—starting with Mayor Charlie Luken, who brought public and private sector leaders together in 2002 to form 3CDC, a redevelopment project for the area. The commitment only grew, so that in 2014 there were many players—from the current mayor John Cranley to the University of Cincinnati and other higher-learning institutions, to the corporations that had a stake there, such as Kroger and Procter & Gamble, to the startup and investment communities that led the way. These included the Brandery, a seed-stage startup accelerator, and Cintrifuse, an organization formed by the Cincinnati Business Committee to spearhead innovation efforts. When we visited, Cintrifuse was in the final stages of completing its first major project, the redevelopment of Over-the-Rhine's Union Hall.

Union Hall is actually three buildings, dating back to before the Civil War, when one of them was a beer hall and then a dance hall, while another was a union meeting place—such as the Horseshoers Union. They're spread over 38,000 feet in the heart of the Over-the-Rhine neighborhood. The new Union Hall opened the year after we visited and quickly became a popular centerpiece of the area. The facility has coworking, event, and office spaces that have helped energize the startup community. Cintrifuse has its headquarters there.

This transformation of Over-the-Rhine from a troubled, crime-ridden neighborhood into a revitalized and rebranded "OTR" that quickly became a magnet for entrepreneurs was striking. My first job out of college was at P&G in Cincinnati, and back then the city had all its focus on a handful of Fortune 500 companies, and the downtown was dead on evenings and weekends. Now it's cool to live downtown, and OTR is a key beneficiary, emerging as a powerful innovation district.

COLUMBUS: Idea Foundry

Alex Bandar has called himself an accidental entrepreneur. An engineer who worked for many years for a software company advising top-end management clients, he became obsessed with making things himself—the way his sister, a sculptor, did. That obsession became a reality with the development of Idea Foundry in 2008, which he dubbed "a clubhouse for makers."

Idea Foundry is housed in a century-old, renovated shoe factory in the Franklinton neighborhood of Columbus, called the Bottoms for the flooding from the abutting Scioto and Olentangy Rivers. People still talk about the great flood of 1913, which killed nearly one hundred people and destroyed much of the community and the downtown area. Ninety-one years later, in 2004, a floodwall was completed to protect the area.

Idea Foundry is an ode to a dynamic tech future, with a massive "makerspace" for electronics, welding, design, 3D printing, and the like, plus an equally large coworking facility with offices for forty businesses and startups.

A big part of the Columbus startup success is the support of some of the city's big guns—companies like Nationwide and State Automobile Mutual Insurance. Public funds have also been available. The year before our Rise of the Rest visit in 2017, the federal government awarded $40 million to Columbus in its Smart City Challenge, which was subsequently turned into a $500 million investment, thanks to private sector investments. As a sign of the impact tech ecosystems can have on the larger community, a number of startups that were developed at Idea Foundry chose to stay in Franklinton. Alex Bandar observed, "Makerspaces can serve as centers of gravity that attract, create, and retain makers, doers, and entrepreneurs."

A confirmation of Columbus's status as a startup hub came in 2018. In consultation with Rise of the Rest, *Forbes* set out to identify which cities were emerging as the top startup cities for the next decade and beyond. Columbus, Ohio, earned the number one spot. *Forbes* cited its low cost of living, low cost of doing business, college support, and the number of venture capital deals since 2013 that showed Columbus was on the rise.

We've heard a similar analysis from founders. Steve Lekas, cofounder of Branch, an innovative community-based insurance startup, described the thorough analytical process they went through before choosing Columbus as their headquarters. Starting with 208 cities in the United States that had more than 150,000 people, they developed a set of criteria. "The biggest was cost of living, which immediately took out Boston, New York, San Francisco, and anywhere in Hawaii," Steve said. "We winnowed it down algorithmically, with things like local talent sets, the attractiveness of recruiting, major universities, size of airport, and so on." Once they narrowed the candidate cities down to twenty-one, they looked at different livability factors for various demographics, and came up with the finalists: Austin, Raleigh, Durham, Nashville, and Columbus. Of those, Columbus checked the most boxes. Since launching in Columbus in 2017, Branch has thrived, raising more than $82 million in funding from a variety of investors, including Rise of the Rest Seed Fund.

In January 2022, Intel announced that it would invest $20 billion to build two semiconductor plants near Columbus and ultimately develop it into the largest semiconductor manufacturing center in the world. The plan is expected to create thousands of jobs and set the stage for a tech windfall in the Midwest. It's just the kind of opening that will bring a massive flow of jobs, talent, and capital to the area.

It's especially meaningful when you consider the history. Intel CEO Pat Gelsinger noted, "We helped create Silicon Valley. We're now going to create Silicon Heartland around Columbus."

FIVE

The Geography of Opportunity

Chattanooga, which we visited on a Rise of the Rest tour in 2018, is a remarkable hidden gem that is on track to emerge as one of America's great entrepreneurial cities. Despite being small, it has something going for it that outpaces other small and medium-sized cities. It has a smart grid—and it's all because of some innovative city administrators. Back in 2009 when there were funds available from the Troubled Assets Relief Program (TARP) for shovel-ready projects, the city of Chattanooga wanted to create a smart grid through its public utility. The city managers realized that in order to have a smart grid they had to have fiber, and then they figured that if they were going to have fiber, they should provide high-speed internet access to the entire population. Chattanooga became the first city to do that, and as a result the city—nicknamed "Gig City"—suddenly had the fastest internet in the country.

It's a big reason why Chattanooga has such momentum as a startup city. Given the Gig City moniker, there has been a lot of interest from tech companies and other new businesses.

Chattanooga has something else going for it too—an engaged mayor, focused on startups. Andy Berke, who served between 2013 and 2021 (and was term limited), came into office with a vigorous plan to get the struggling city on its feet. In 2015 he announced the creation of the Innovation District.

The Innovation District has sparked a number of advantages that are welcoming to the startup community. The Tomorrow Building is such an effort. When Lamp Post Group, a local venture capital firm, found that it was having trouble attracting and retaining good people to Chattanooga, it determined that a big part of the challenge was finding suitable high-quality housing and amenities for workers coming from larger cities. The VC firm decided to redevelop an existing building into the Tomorrow Building, and position it as the "landing pad" for people moving to Chattanooga. The units are all furnished so someone moving in doesn't need to bring much more than their personal belongings. There are communal kitchens and lots of organized activities. This might be a model for a boomerang era, as more young people looking to relocate want to land in a place where there is a built-in community. What Chattanooga understands is that communities have to provide substantive amenities to attract workers, especially if they want them to stay.

Regions and cities with specialized institutional knowledge are being enabled to generate startups to take advantage of domain expertise—meaning they're the best places to support particular industries. The blanket presumption that tech companies are better off in Silicon Valley has been replaced by the realization that some companies are actually better off because they're *not* in Silicon Valley.

CREATING FREIGHT ALLEY IN CHATTANOOGA

When Craig Fuller, the Chattanooga founder of FreightWaves, made the case to be included in the Rise of the Rest pitch competition in 2018, he declared, "Chattanooga is Freight Alley—welcome!" We were impressed, and we didn't know at the time that Craig had just coined that term for our benefit. He was putting a name to a dynamic that was very much happening in the small city of Chattanooga.

"We're building on Chattanooga's natural resources, human talent, and existing businesses," Craig said. "We've created a freight logistics startup that takes the talent that's already here and builds something. Logistics is a job that people really respect. It's a destination job in Chattanooga. I think the problem for logistics in bigger cities is that people don't understand how much money and respect it garners. One of the advantages of being a small community is that focus. It's the equivalent of working in social media in Palo Alto."

If Chattanooga is Freight Alley, it's in part due to the contribution of Craig's family. "My grandfather was a patriarch of long-haul trucking," Craig told us. "He was one of the first to put two people into a truck and drive across the country when the interstates were popping up." Craig's dad followed his father into the business, starting a trucking company of his own, which today is the fifth largest in the nation. And his brother-in-law started a trucking company that is the eighth largest in the nation. So, the family has roots.

"If you have a founder as a dad, the way to spend time with him is to really know what he clicks with," Craig said. "Some kids spend time with their dads hunting. Others spend time riding four-wheelers or mountain biking or going hiking. My dad just happened to be in trucking, so that's how I spent time with him and became really familiar with the business. When Dad took his company public in 1994, I wanted to learn how the stock market worked, because it was a big event in our family. I idolized my dad. My dream was to be my dad in some ways. And so I learned how the trucking business worked and how the stock market worked."

After college, Craig was attracted to entrepreneurial pursuits, and started TransCard, a fleet payment processor, which he folded into his dad's company. The two locked horns when the company was facing a capital crunch—what Craig describes as the impossible friction when two founders are each trying to take the lead—and his father fired him. "It was a really tough situation because this heroic person in my life had fired me. The only person that I cared about getting approval from had turned on me. I realized I had to figure out my life, but it took me a while to get back on my feet."

Craig dropped off the grid and away from the comfort zone of Chattanooga, moving to Fort Worth where he worked various jobs—unsuccessfully—before he came up with a new business idea in 2016, a logistics data company, which he called FreightWaves. The motivation behind the idea was frustration with the opaqueness of the trucking market. As he explained it, "It's a fragmented market with hundreds of thousands of individual trucking companies, and millions of people that are buying trucking services. And because it's so fragmented and the top ten trucking companies combined have only about 12 percent market share, nobody has comprehensive information on what's happening."

Craig began to build a plan for his logistics company, in the process burning through most of his available cash. In a sense he was writing his own comeback story—recovering from failure by building something stronger. Soon he was discovering that being in Fort Worth—outside the center of trucking—put him at a disadvantage. He had problems hiring experienced people there, and he found that his idea didn't resonate as it might in a place that truly understood and was engaged with the trucking industry. In Chattanooga there had been successful freight startups to point to, including a successful exit.

Soon Craig was packing his bags and moving back home. The timing felt right. He saw it as Chattanooga's real moment to create an entrepreneurial ecosystem because so much capital was available and so many companies were related to freight and logistics. But in 2017, when he talked about it publicly with the mayor, the chamber of commerce, and the local media, highlighting the concentration of logistics talent in Chattanooga, he hit a wall. "Everybody looked at me a little strange," he said. "The chamber of commerce had hired this consultant out of Austin who did a survey, listing the top growth industries to 2050. Logistics wasn't on the list.

"I said, 'Why don't you have logistics jobs on the list? I don't get it.' And they said, 'Well, when we did the survey, there were only like four hundred people who worked in logistics in Chattanooga.' And I looked at them and said, 'There are two thousand jobs represented in this room that are tied to the industry—just in this room!'" Then he started laying it out, talking about the logistics jobs in local companies, such as US Xpress and Covenant. "You guys don't know what the hell you're talking about," he told them with brutal honesty. "You're using government data that doesn't properly reflect what's going on, instead of finding out what's happening here in your own city."

Craig's activism lit a fire, and the city decided it was going to take aggressive action. It hosted a meeting with seventy companies from across the state, representing up to nine thousand employees. Mayors and the chambers of commerce were also invited. It was the first time that freight-related businesses had ever come together as an industry. The business community and the press took note. They had turned a corner in getting the word out.

When Craig heard about Rise of the Rest, he thought, "This is our story. This is an old-school industry where access is really important." He was very much aware of being a part of the ecosystem, passed down to him from his grandfather and father (whom he was now on good terms with again). He benefited from the wisdom and principles his dad had instilled in him. "I traded on that," he acknowledged. When he won the Rise of the Rest pitch competition, he saw it as a seal of approval.

At that point, FreightWaves had already raised money and closed a Series A funding round, and the greatest benefit of Rise of the Rest also investing was not the money but the local credibility. "It was not so much how the world saw us as how Chattanooga saw us," Craig emphasized. "It was a city that had this really awesome opportunity to become a leader in a sector. When the Rise of the Rest judges gave us the award it sent a message to the rest of the people in the town that this is a model for venture."

NORTHWEST ARKANSAS:
From Walmart Town to Magnet Town

In 1950, a young entrepreneur and variety-store owner named Sam Walton bought a store in Bentonville, Arkansas, and named it Walton's 5 & 10 Variety Store. There he began to perfect a unique business philosophy: to give customers the best price possible on products while offering a level of service that was unprecedented at the time. In 1962, Walton took another leap and opened Wal-Mart Discount City eight miles away in Rogers. The rest is history.

Bentonville became Walton Town, with Walmart the dominant employer for the area. And Walmart grew rapidly, eventually becoming the largest company in the world, with $500 billion in revenue, and more than two million employees. The Waltons became one of America's wealthiest families and launched a series of philanthropic initiatives.

A particular passion was the desire to transform their hometown into a place that would be a magnet for talent, bringing millennials and young families to northwest Arkansas. The Walton Foundation created the Heartland Forward initiative, and the Heartland Summit. And the Walton family started investing in museums, hotels, restaurants, bike parks, and other appealing local amenities. (Members of the Walton family also invest in the Rise of the Rest Seed Fund.)

Today, northwest Arkansas is becoming an unexpected startup center in the heartland. The work of the Walton family has created momentum and a sense of possibility that has long evaded this corner of the United States. Along with a new economic vitality is a burgeoning arts and culture scene. People are paying attention to what it means to shape all facets of a community—a dynamic referred to as "placemaking." These efforts are buttressed by an overall commitment by northwest Arkansas business leaders to attract top talent to the area. The business community is committed to talent development, with appealing initiatives such as cash incentives for new residents and lifestyle perks such as mountain bike giveaways so new residents can explore over three hundred miles of bike trails.

With a burgeoning entrepreneurial emphasis, Arkansas, with the support of the Walton Foundation, has launched the Heartland Challenge, a global startup competition for graduate student entrepreneurs. Because of the pandemic, the challenge, held in May 2020, was a virtual event, featuring twelve international teams for the semifinals and finals. I was proud to be on hand to present the awards. The winners included some exciting startups: first place went to Aurign, a Georgia State University startup using blockchain technology to securely file music publishing documents; second place was AlgenAir, a University of Maryland–sponsored company dedicated to improving air quality; and third place was CelluDot, a University of Arkansas startup designed to eliminate herbicide drift.

It's very meaningful to have a major international startup competition centered in Arkansas—a sign that a part of the country that had struggled in the new tech economy is coming into its own. In late 2021, the Dallas-based electric vehicle startup Canoo announced that it was moving its headquarters to Bentonville, heralding a new generation of tech opportunity in a bedrock town.

Another transplant is Jessica Matthews, the editor of *Fortune* magazine's *Term Sheet* newsletter, which covers the world of venture capital. Who would have thought that the latest developments in innovation capitals like Silicon Valley would be chronicled from a desk in Bentonville, Arkansas?

A Founder Seeks Farmland Revival

Carter Malloy was born in Little Rock, but his family's farm was in Stuttgart, Arkansas, forty-five miles away. There he spent much of his childhood out on the Grand Prairie—"a big, flat, beautiful part of the world." Love of the farming community was ingrained in him, so when he went to work for a hedge fund in San Francisco after college, a big part of his focus was buying and selling farmland. He achieved some great financial outcomes, but his transaction experience was terrible.

Carter realized there was very little information to guide investors, and the market was dominated by a large number of very small (often just one or two people) local brokerage firms that would represent local sellers and connect them to local buyers. "It's a hyperlocal market," Carter said, "and just incredibly difficult to transact on either side due to lack of access, lack of transparency, and lack of liquidity."

For years Carter played with the idea of starting a farmland investment fund, hoping to improve the system. When he began to do research, he was stunned by what he found. "This was a multi-trillion-dollar asset class, and there's no modern capital formation here, there is no real technological innovation. Whereas over on the residential real estate side, it seems like there's a new billion-dollar company every week."

Over the course of a year, while Carter worked his day job, he devoted evenings to creating a business plan, with the help of his dad and some friends. When he was far enough along, he hired technologists to build the product.

Carter planned to move home to Arkansas in 2018 for the launch of his startup, which he called AcreTrader. "It sounded crazy—leaving San Francisco to start a technology company in

Fayetteville, Arkansas," he acknowledged. That was especially true when you consider he was leaving a lucrative career and had a family to support. He decided the risk was worth it. "I felt that it was really important we be close to the farmland in the middle of the country. Also, although Fayetteville is small—half a million people—it's where the University of Arkansas is, and it's where some huge employers, like Walmart, Tyson, and J.B. Hunt are. Such a great workforce for building a company."

However, from the outset Carter learned some of the hard-knock lessons of starting a company. "It was a monstrous learning experience," he said. The first lesson was that there is a big difference between feedback and results. When Carter told people about the concept, the response was overwhelmingly positive. But when he pitched investors, the number of people who were willing to show up and invest money was, in his words, "staggeringly none." He determined that there were two barriers—education and trust. He was introducing a new asset class, and it would take time.

"It's a big ask," he acknowledged, "to ask a farmer to trust us with their land, or a landowner to trust us with their land. And that is a work in progress. We're lucky to have a huge database of investors that have expressed trust in us and work with us. But I think that phase of the business, that trust building phase, was where I really learned the rule: don't do things that don't scale. In the early days of any startup, you want to build the business and you want to build the chassis around this idea of scalability."

It was a struggle for AcreTrader to raise seed capital, hire a team, secure initial partners, and be taken seriously in the community. But being in Arkansas also proved to be a huge advantage, because Carter's local roots, and his decision to headquarter the company in Fayetteville, not San Francisco, went a long way toward building trust. Carter was known in the community, and his decision to build locally inspired confidence that he was sincere about helping farmers succeed.

Carter believes that the best sign of his growing success is the ability to attract people from Boulder, Dallas, Seattle, Austin, New York, and Chicago to live and work in Arkansas. "They come from everywhere and they absolutely love it," he said. "It's a wonderful place to call home."

Investors have finally woken up to the opportunity. Carter has raised more than $50 million, making AcreTrader one of the best capitalized startups in Arkansas. And his momentum is beginning to change the perception of Arkansas and encourage other entrepreneurs to take their own shots and pursue their own dreams.

"Farming has always been a challenging profession," Carter said realistically. "You can look at articles about agriculture in the nineteenth century, and it was a challenge. It is a commodity-production business, so it is an inherently difficult one. But we bring money to rural communities, and that is a good thing."

SPACE COAST: Home to Outer Space

Our last Rise of the Rest bus tour before the pandemic took us to Florida's Space Coast, where moonshots are made. Growing up, I was a product of my generation, obsessed with the miracle of space travel. I was eleven years old during the Apollo mission, when American astronauts landed on the moon. I can remember thinking, "Wow, if we did this, we can do anything!" I still marvel that we accomplished the impossible.

I have no doubt that the moon launch had a life-altering effect on my generation. We witnessed it and learned to say, "Don't tell me we can't do anything we set our minds to. We've already done it!"

The promise of space had another impact on young kids like me. It kept us focused on the future—on what we one day might become. I've thought of it many times during my career and drawn lessons from it.

In the case of Rise of the Rest's visit to the Space Coast, the "hometown" was the universe—or at least the nation. Our pitch competition was open to anyone in the United States working in space, drone, or aviation technology, or in related industries.

We arrived on the bus on April 30, 2019, and for that day our imaginations were lifted by the vastness of opportunity and the rich history of America's journeys to space. Every stop on the tour was a thrill, especially starting the day at the Kennedy Space Center beneath the space shuttle *Atlantis*. The rest of the day, we visited labs testing food that could be grown in space, designers and manufacturers producing satellites for low Earth orbit, and a tech center filled with space-loving students.

We ended up investing in several companies we met during our Space Coast visit, including Hermeus, which is building hypersonic aircraft in Atlanta. That initially struck me as an odd place to build Mach 5 technology, but—as is often the case when we visit rising cities—the founder AJ Piplica had a strategic reason for locating in Georgia, not California. He wanted to tap into the engineering talent at Georgia Tech, one of the largest research universities in the country. After our initial investment, Hermeus went on to sign a $60 million development agreement with the U.S. Air Force and was well on its way to building its hypersonic engine.

In March 2022, Rise of the Rest joined investor Sam Altman, the Founders Fund, In-Q-Tel, and others in a $100 million Series B funding round. Hermeus announced that the investment would be used to complete the development of Quarterhorse, its first aircraft, and accelerate development of its next aircraft Darkhorse—an uncrewed aircraft capable of sustained hypersonic flight. With the announcement, Trae Stephens, a partner at Founders Fund, said, "Hermeus is the hypersonics company the country needs right now—the right people, moving incredibly fast, and building for both commercial and defense markets."

The winner of the Space Coast pitch competition was Vanessa Clark, a Denver aerospace engineer who founded Atomos Space, which she described as "the railroad of space"—high-powered electric propulsion space tugs, which can move satellites to any orbit beyond the low Earth orbit.

Vanessa hails from Australia and was trained there, obtaining physics/mathematics undergraduate and graduate degrees in aerospace engineering and management. She then relocated to Colorado as the principal propulsion engineer and manager at Lockheed Martin. But over time she came to believe that she couldn't solve the big problems she wanted to solve working for a space agency or a large space company. For that she needed to carve her own path and become an entrepreneur.

Vanessa's concept was to design a way to remove the barriers to accessing space that she had experienced in her work. This was a purpose that captured our imaginations at Rise of the Rest because we were on a similar mission on Earth! We were inspired by the idea of open access to space and Vanessa's goal of developing the technologies that will enable humans to access space beyond Earth orbit. "We change crazy space logistics, incredibly wasteful and inefficient, into how we do logistics on the ground today," Vanessa explained.

Getting the idea off the ground was a daunting task. The regulatory environment alone could discourage most people from even considering a space company. And how do you raise money for such a long-term project?

Vanessa and her husband, William, who is her business partner, had liquidated their 401(k)s, maxed out their credit cards, borrowed from family, and were nearly out of money when Atomos won the Rise of the Rest pitch competition. That win helped them get over the line.

Although we met Vanessa at Space Coast for a national competition, she is deeply embedded in the startup community in Denver, with no plan of moving. "Interesting statistic," Vanessa said. "Colorado has more aerospace engineers per capita than any other state. We don't have a NASA center, but we do have the Air Force Academy. We have a lot of space and defense contractors, like United Launch Alliance, Sierra Aerospace, and Lockheed Martin, where I used to work. It's really an aerospace hub that people don't know about. So, Colorado brings that together with affordability and a great quality of life. It also has the talent base that we need and the partnership and customer base that makes sense."

In addition to a very promising and ultimately lucrative space product, Vanessa and William hope to play a positive role in building support for space companies like Atomos. It really is the next frontier. They like to imagine a future in which their grandkids see the Starfleet taking off, as they had watched on *Star Trek*, and say, "My grandparents built that."

SIX

Big City Reimagination

The Freedom Tower at Miami Dade College has been a beacon on the skyline since 1925. Once the South's tallest building, it stood as a welcome to those who came by land or by sea. During the 1960s, refugees escaping the Cuban Revolution were processed there, and it later became a monument to the Cuban American experience. After being acquired by Miami Dade College it became an art museum and cultural center, reflecting Miami's diversity and vitality.

It was fitting that Rise of the Rest opened our Miami tour with a community breakfast at the Freedom Tower. We were joined by then–Miami Dade College president Eduardo Padron, who was born in Cuba and came to the United States as a refugee at age fifteen. Also there was Miami mayor Francis Suarez. Suarez's father, Xavier, who was born in Cuba, served two terms as mayor before him. It was great to see these leaders gather together and proclaim, *This is a moment. Let's seize it. Let's really focus on startups. Let's be a magnet for the talent. Then we can be a magnet for the capital.*

The diverse spirit of Miami was on display with every stop on our tour, as leaders proudly heralded it as a city founded and built by immigrants—adding that in many cases it was led by women. The statistics are impressive—52 percent of the Miami population is foreign-born, and it's one of the leading metro areas for immigrant-owned businesses.

A clear leader of entrepreneurial vitality is Manuel Medina, one of Miami's most prolific and successful tech entrepreneurs and investors and the founder of Medina Capital. Born in Cuba, he came to the United States at age thirteen. After achieving tremendous success himself, he shifted his focus to helping others succeed. I first met Manny through his program eMerge, which was fast becoming a model of tech ecosystem development. The centerpiece of the program is an annual conference that brings together thousands of attendees from around the world. I was invited to participate in the 2016 eMerge conference and talk about the Third Wave and how to encourage startups. I was impressed by the attendance—more than fifteen thousand attendees representing four hundred companies and forty countries. More than one hundred startups participated in a Startup Showcase competition. "eMerge started as a dream," Manny told the crowd, "to be a platform where leaders of technology from all over the world gather, where CEOs do a lot of business, where the next leading innovator gets his lead investor and [where] technology brings thousands of people from all over the world to Miami and help propel Miami into this technology world we live in."

Manny's daughter Melissa, eMerge's president, is an impressive example of a new generation of leadership. Melissa credits her immigrant parents for modeling an entrepreneurial drive. "They both came here with nothing and didn't know the language, and they built a successful life, and I believe that spirit is ingrained in my DNA," she said.

In addition, working alongside her entrepreneurial father in his real estate company gave Melissa invaluable tools. "From a very young age, I was sitting in the boardroom with him," she recalled. "I was working in the summer, even as a teenager, on due diligence projects and absorbing as much as I could about building a business."

Melissa continued to work for her father in the summers during her college years before leaving to do a master's at the global management school ESADE in Barcelona. She had intended to move to New York after graduation, but 9/11 changed things. She'd always thought she'd return to Miami eventually, but the terrorist attacks accelerated her plans. She came home.

It so happened that her return coincided with her father transitioning his real estate company Terremark into a tech company. She was there to get in on the ground floor. "That was my introduction to technology," Melissa said. "I remember that many of my father's partners were calling me to say that my father was crazy for selling his real estate assets and putting all his eggs in this technology basket. But having grown up with my dad, I always told them I believed in him one hundred percent—and it was like the famous words of Steve Jobs: 'The people who are crazy enough to think they can change the world are the ones who do.' I feel like those words were basically written about my dad. So that's where my love for technology started."

In 2011, Terremark was purchased by Verizon. It was a pivotal moment for the ecosystem—a great tech success story from an immigrant founder that set the stage for the next venture, eMerge, which Melissa cofounded with her father.

The eMerge conferences have been a great success for an important reason. "The heart and soul of eMerge has been our connection with entrepreneurs and with a startup ecosystem," Melissa emphasized. "And that's always been top of mind from the beginning. If we can connect startups with investors, if we can connect startups with potential talent, or if we can connect startups with potential partners, and they succeed, then our ecosystem is going to succeed."

It seems to be working, and Melissa is enthusiastic about the progress. "It's really exciting to hear so many people excited about Miami tech and the Miami tech ecosystem. And I think we have a real opportunity to leverage that excitement. We have an influx of not only financial capital, but intellectual capital that's coming from around the country and the world. And we've only scratched the surface."

After my eMerge visit in 2016, Rise of the Rest kept in touch with the startup scene in Miami, which was developing at a rapid pace. I continued to be impressed by its attention to diversity and inclusion and its respect for the immigrant experience. Most interesting, the leadership was positioning Miami not only as a state and regional tech hub but also as an international tech city. Like Melissa Medina, eMerge's CEO, Felice Gorordo, was an example of a new generation of leadership. I'd first met Felice in 2012 when I served on the President's Council on Jobs and Competitiveness. Felice, the son of immigrants, was a White House aide working on immigration policy. Now he had returned home to be part of the thriving startup scene in Miami. He immediately began lobbying Rise of the Rest to bring the tour there and we did in 2019.

Following our opening breakfast at the Freedom Tower, we hit some of Miami's startup highlights, including the Miami Animation and Gaming International Complex (MAGIC) at

Miami Dade College and a demonstration by Magic Leap, a wearable technology startup in Plantation, thirty miles outside of Miami, that had raised almost $2 billion and relocated four hundred families from Silicon Valley to Florida.

At our fireside chat later in the day we noted that Miami was the most inclusive city we had visited on our tours. A female founder, Lil Roberts, won the pitch competition with her small-business bookkeeping startup, Xendoo. Her inspiring story of thriving against the odds was an example of what Rise of the Rest's mission is all about.

The pandemic proved to be helpful for the Miami startup system. A number of venture capitalists relocated to Miami, and Silicon Valley–based Founders Fund opened an office there. All of this makes Mayor Suarez even more bullish on future opportunity, including making Miami the capital of crypto. He is also intent on attracting talent to the city. In 2021, a giant billboard appeared above a central road near the Twitter headquarters in San Francisco. The message, above Suarez's Twitter address, read: "Thinking of moving to Miami? DM me."

A Story of Founder Tenacity

Lil Roberts grew up poor in South Florida, the fourth of five siblings. In the space of a decade, she lost her father and three of her brothers. She was twenty when her favorite brother died, and at that moment she decided that she was going to wring everything she could out of life because she couldn't count on it lasting. Her aspirations were simple. "I started working full-time when I was fourteen to help contribute to the family because the last two weeks of the month, we didn't eat so well," she explained. "I wanted to get to a point that I could eat anything I wanted to eat, and when I went to the grocery store, I didn't have to calculate what was in the basket." The experience of going hungry stayed with her, to the point that she's incorporated weekly lunches, holiday meals, and monthly birthday cakes into her business to make sure everyone has something to eat and a friendly support system.

Lil didn't have an opportunity to go to college, but she did go to a trade school where she learned electronics. She went to work at National Cash Register and excelled at every job she had, eventually striking out on her own and becoming a serial entrepreneur. Along the way, she helped many local entrepreneurs evaluate the potential of their business plans, creating a scorecard.

In 2016, when she had an idea for a startup, she used the scorecard on herself. She knew she wanted to help small business owners, and she wanted the experience of founding a venture-backed company. "I thought it would stretch me as a human being and it would make me stretch my mind," she said. With the advice of friends and colleagues in the local entrepreneurial community, she devised her plan for an online bookkeeping and accounting company that would solve small business owners' problems and give them a support system. She market tested her company, Xendoo, at the nearby Pompano Festival Flea Market. The sign said "No Solicitors," and she ignored it and started talking to the vendors. "I lasted forty-five minutes before the guard kicked me out," she said and laughed. It was enough time to get very positive feedback and a couple of new clients.

The first big test of Lil's business idea was at the eMerge pitch competition, where Xendoo was accepted as one of the finalists. Before she went on stage, an investor told her bluntly,

"You won't win. You're older, you're a female, and you're from Broward County." She was determined to prove him wrong, and she did by winning. The following year when Rise of the Rest was coming to town, she was encouraged to enter our pitch competition. She found the process incredibly rigorous— "like going from playing college football to the NFL"—and she felt extremely humbled by the level of the competition.

After Lil won the Rise of the Rest competition, she became even more dedicated to giving back to the Miami ecosystem. She really got what we were about with Rise of the Rest—as she described it, "planting seeds with as many founders as possible from areas that don't traditionally get funding and helping those founders grow businesses, helping keep the people from leaving—growing up in an area, going to college somewhere else and never coming back."

A few months after our tour in Miami, the pandemic hit. Lil was undaunted. She sent her people to work from home, but she came alone to work in the office every day—for mental health reasons. "I needed to see the world moving in order to be able to live through it." Her office was facing I-95, and at lunch she'd get a bowl of soup from the café downstairs, and she'd stand at the window and look out at I-95 and eat her soup. "I would watch what kind of cars were on the road," she said. "And what that told me is who was still doing the work. I'd see all these trucks with ladders and determined that the trade services were not getting as affected. I needed to reach out to them and make them my customers."

DALLAS: Innovation in D-Town

At first, our 2018 tour of Dallas seemed to be the story of two worlds, but in the course of a day we found those worlds coming together into the possibility of one diverse ecosystem. Our day began at Old Parkland, a historic hospital that had been renovated as a center of business and culture. The breakfast included some of the most influential people in the city—Harlan Crow, chairman of Crow Holdings; Ron Kirk, former Dallas mayor and US trade representative; Andre Fuetsch, president of AT&T Labs and AT&T's chief technology officer; Jennifer Sampson, CEO of the United Way of Metropolitan Dallas; Dale Petroskey, president and CEO of the Dallas Regional Chamber; Rob Kaplan, Federal Reserve Bank of Dallas president and CEO; and Richard Benson, president of the University of Texas at Dallas.

We saw it as an opportunity to bring together some of the most powerful people in Dallas, which is a large city with a tremendous amount of wealth, and get them to focus on innovation and entrepreneurship and the power of startups.

Afterward, we asked some of them to join us on the bus for a stop in a very different kind of neighborhood—Paul Quinn College in South Dallas, an area that most of them typically didn't visit.

Paul Quinn College, under the direction of its president Michael Sorrell, was a surprising startup story. When Sorrell took over in 2001, the historic Black college was nearly bankrupt, with rapidly declining registration and income. There was a big question about whether it would survive. Sorrell knew he had to do something bold and take a big risk. He saw that he needed not only to attract new students and save the school but also to get the community involved. So even though this was

Texas, where football is sacrosanct, he tore up the football field and turned it into an urban farm. Visualize a *Friday Night Lights* football stadium in Texas, and now it's covered in kale.

Imagine the phenomenal act of audacity for this small HBCU president to declare, in effect, "Forget football. We don't have food. We don't have jobs." As Sorrell liked to say with pride, "We send more lettuce to the Dallas Cowboys than we do football players."

In fighting for the future of the college, Sorrell understands that he is also battling poverty. By transforming the school into an urban work college, he has given it new life and provided fresh opportunity to the students, many of whom are poor. In the reorganized work-study environment, every student is required to have a job.

When we reached the college, our bus got stuck making the turn into the narrow driveway. We got off the bus and hoofed it in the blazing early afternoon heat, as Michael Sorrell hurried down to greet us. He invited us to walk along with him, and we soon arrived at what used to be the football field—still backed by the old scoreboard—which was now a large active farm. Sorrell began to introduce us to students working the farm, and they were all eager to talk to us—some of them even joined us on the bus for the rest of our day. These were aspiring entrepreneurs who were excited to see us. They were proud of their entrepreneurial chops—learning what it actually meant to build and innovate in a food desert.

"This feels like it's a moment," I had told the breakfast group at Old Parkland. "Dallas is on the rise, but it could be doing even better." By better I meant forming a more cohesive ecosystem—one where the movers in different parts of the city knew each other and supported each other's efforts. It was clear to me when we went to Paul Quinn College that hardly anyone who'd joined us on the bus had ever been there before. This was a learning opportunity—a chance to do what we do, which involves hosting important conversations in unexpected places. It's a core premise of Rise of the Rest. If everybody goes to the same place where they always convene to talk about the same things with the same group of people, we haven't catalyzed anything through the tours.

We wanted to bring all areas together because Dallas is a thriving city, full of potential—one of the fastest-growing metropolitan areas in the country.

I was interested in an observation made by local entrepreneur Amber Venz Box during our fireside chat later in the day. Amber created the startup RewardStyle and LikeToKnowIt with her husband, Baxter, which monetizes fashion blogging. She recounted how hard she worked to get approval from the established business community, and how difficult that was. "That's the cool thing about technology today," she said. "You don't need anyone's approval to be able to do it. No longer do those hierarchies hold." (Incidentally, RewardStyle has thrived, recently becoming a unicorn company.)

Our pitch competition took place at the Community Beer Co., a craft brewery and events hub in downtown Dallas. The winner was Cameron Johnson, the Black founder of Nickson, a furniture rental startup that takes the hassle out of moving.

A Texas Founder Disrupts Real Estate

Cameron Johnson didn't always think of himself as an entrepreneur, but he had an entrepreneur's sensibility. After graduating from Harvard Business School, he joined a firm called Greystar

Real Estate Partners, one of the largest apartment managers in the nation. He described his role working directly for the CEO and COO as a "strategic sharpshooter," who handled the challenge of turning over tens of thousands of apartments across the country. He noticed that potential renters frequently asked if they could rent the staged model apartment, furniture and all. He asked himself, "If people are asking to rent the model, why? And why is the answer no?"

People wanted to simplify the move-in experience because they were renting and moving more than ever, especially following the 2008 financial crisis. The average was a move every two years. And people hated moving. On the stress meter, it was right up there with divorce or the death of a loved one. And although many renters were attracted to the model apartments, they weren't interested in going to furniture rental companies, which were expensive, considered lowbrow, and only provided limited items. Instead, they went to IKEA, which Cameron described as "moving squared." Not only did you have to furnish the place; you had to *build* your furniture.

Cameron's plan was to create a way for renters to add everything they needed to a space in the same way they added cable. And by everything, he meant a comprehensive list, right down to the laundry basket, shower caddy, and hangers. His company, Nickson, would be in the "everything business." The design and quality would be similar to what people bought themselves, sourcing from vendors like Wayfair, West Elm, and Target, and it would all be affordable with a monthly fee.

Better still, Nickson would handle the move, showing up in advance and getting the keys from the manager, cleaning the space, putting everything in place including art on the walls, and returning the keys. The move-in experience would be as simple as walking in the front door.

To test his concept, Cameron walked around his Dallas neighborhood trying to convince landlords to turn over their most distressed apartments with a promise that he'd transform them. Even though he was offering to do it at no cost, he didn't get any takers. But a friend's family owned a building in Philadelphia that was not fully occupied, and they were willing to give Cameron a shot at one of the two-bedroom apartments. He moved everything he needed to Philadelphia over a long Labor Day weekend, and went to work, painting, putting the furniture together, stocking the kitchen shelves, and hanging art on the walls. It was ready to go the day after the holiday.

The test apartment had been priced at $1,500 a month and had gone unrented for a long time. Within four days of Cameron's transformation, the apartment rented for $2,000 a month for eighteen months. The property manager responded, "Oh my God, this kid is on to something."

By then Cameron was working with the Dallas Entrepreneurship Center (DEC) to launch Nickson, which simplified the process through an app. There he found a host of resources he didn't even know he needed until he got going—web designers, business developers, VC funding advisers—all leading up to his entry in the Rise of the Rest Dallas tour pitch competition for which he was selected as one of ten finalists.

When he stood up to give his pitch at the Community Beer Co., Cameron displayed an old picture from the mid-1700s showing a man driving an overloaded horse and buggy, his possessions stacked in a towering heap behind him. Imagine a time, he said, when people had to carry all of their possessions with them when they moved. Now imagine the opposite of that—where your possessions are there waiting for you.

Cameron won the Dallas pitch competition and received the $100,000 Rise of the Rest investment. "It was credentializing, to say the least," he said. "It changed the game." He then won the Harvard Business School New Venture competition, for the Midwest region. "So those two things basically said, 'People smarter than you, Cameron, are saying this is a good idea. So maybe it's a good idea.'"

The coming years would underscore the point, with Nickson growing rapidly. In 2021, Nickson closed on a successful Series A funding round, which Rise of the Rest joined, led by Pendulum, an investment firm started by Robbie Robinson, who after a career at Goldman Sachs moved on to help Byron Trott start BDT Capital in Chicago, and then worked for President Obama to set up an investment office for him after he left the White House. Robbie, a graduate of Morehouse College, was passionate about backing underrepresented founders, so Nickson was a great fit. Backstage Capital, a VC firm led by Arlan Hamilton with a similar focus on helping underrepresented founders, also joined us in the funding round.

Cameron appreciates the wisdom of starting Nickson in Dallas, where all the advantages are aligned. The weather cooperates, the landscape makes moving easier. And the attitude matters too—"this grit and cowboy mentality that Dallas has. People are supportive. It's God's country. The message is, 'If that's what God's put in your heart and that's what he gave you the talent to do, you go for it, and you take your shot. And I hope you have a blessed day.' That's the culture of Dallas."

Two Friends Tackle the Caring Industry

There are so many meaningful founder stories in every city we visit. Here's one more that highlights the Dallas startup ecosystem. It's the story of Cariloop, started by cofounders who actually moved to Dallas from the Midwest after researching the potential for health care startups there.

Michael Walsh and Steven Theesfeld were childhood buddies. "We played Little League baseball together," Michael said. "We went to grade school and high school together. I was the best man at his wedding. And he was the officiant at mine. We're lifelong friends, brothers, partners, teammates."

They also had in common the desire to start something that would make a footprint on the world. And life intervened to show them what that footprint would be. In 2005, shortly before he got married, Steve's father-in-law was diagnosed with terminal cancer. "He didn't even make it to the wedding—that's how quickly he went," Michael recalled. "But when you're dealing with a cancer diagnosis and all that comes with it, it certainly is illuminating in terms of what people go through and how challenging it is."

Michael, too, was having a rough time. In 2008, as the economy was crashing, Michael was working hard at his job at a management consulting firm in Chicago. Then his maternal grandfather got very sick. Michael is the oldest of five, with four younger sisters. Michael's mother, who was normally home, had to spend time over the next several years helping to care for her dad. As a result, Michael accepted extra responsibilities to take over the business and care for his young sisters, who were in grade school. So, at the age of twenty-three, he got to see a lot of what went on with families that were dealing with devastating health crises.

In early 2010, Michael had dinner with his old friend Steve. Steve had an idea to build software that would help families understand the range of health provider options and make the right decisions. Over the next two years they worked on the concept, which would ultimately become Cariloop. "We had no idea what we were doing, we had no idea how to start a business or build a technology platform, or certainly no experience going out there and creating something from scratch," Michael said. "But we were very motivated and very inspired by what we'd gone through. And each of us was seeing what was going on with other families as a result of the work we were doing professionally. The system itself needed some drastic overhauls as it relates to the way that it supported families and caregivers after they discharged patients. We said, 'Let's see if we can figure out a solution to this.'"

As the idea headed toward reality, they began to think about location. They brought an unusual degree of intentionality to the task. Since their startup would be linking with hospital and nursing home networks, they began with calls to trade associations across the country representing hospitals and nursing homes. Michael remembered one call in particular. "We ended up on the phone with a group in Texas, and we shared our idea. They loved it. And they said, 'Hey, if you will come down to our annual conference in San Antonio in July, and buy a booth at the conference, you can exhibit and meet our members. We'll give you fifteen minutes at our board meeting to present your idea and get some feedback.'"

They headed down, and were impressed by the enthusiastic reception they received. "That's something that we've seen consistently with the Texas community at large," Michael said.

"There is a bootstrap mentality and a help-a-fellow-neighbor-out mindset here that we didn't see in some other markets we were contacting."

They also found it to be a fantastic health care market and a compelling place to start a business. "You've got great weather, low cost of living, tons of talent," he said. "But honestly it was the culture and the people and just how much energy and enthusiasm there was for new ideas. And just that hustle mentality. It was infectious."

So they took the leap and launched Cariloop in Texas. Michael moved to Dallas and Steve to Austin. The first year was a struggle and lonely, but Michael connected with Tech Wildcatters, a well-established accelerator. Better still, it spun off into Health Wildcatters and Michael found his community.

"I was probably the first to apply for Health Wildcatters back in 2013 when it was announced and set up," Michael said. "I went through their program, and that helped attract our first investors. That lit the match and gave us some financial horsepower. We increased our sales efforts to secure employers as customers, but it was hard. Most employers thought this was something that was already covered by an insurance program or Medicare. Employers didn't see it as their responsibility back then.

"That forced us to pivot. There was some early research starting to come out about what was going on with caregivers and the impact that it had on them from a physical, financial, mental, social, and spiritual standpoint. So, we pressed reset and said we're going to build the world's first tech-enabled, human-powered caregiver support platform. And instead of being a marketplace where you can find services and providers, it's going to be all about pairing you with a licensed or certified professional (or a "Care Coach") that comes from a medical or health care background.

"This Care Coach goes on the whole journey with you and helps you balance your work and family responsibilities. We completely reengineered and reimagined the software experience, placing the caregiver and the Care Coach at the hub of the system, and acknowledging that most caregivers would be on this journey for years.

"It's our vision to put the caregiver at the center," Michael said. "Without the caregiver, the patient, the provider, the payer cannot thrive."

Michael introduces a big reality check about building the business and needing to pivot. It was challenging to basically start over from scratch at that point, especially since they were just scraping by. "I think my Cariloop W2s between 2012, when we were founded, and 2018 probably average somewhere around $12,000 a year," Michael confessed. "At one point I got certified to be a personal trainer, just to make some extra money to keep the lights on, and I borrowed money from friends and family that I paid back when I could. People don't realize how hard the startup journey is. We live in the *Shark Tank* culture with all the glitz and glamour, and people don't understand what happens underneath and how lonely and how stressful and how challenging it can be, especially when you've got families that are counting on you and people that are invested in your success."

Cariloop was beginning to get traction by the time the pandemic hit, and the need for the service increased overnight. Many families were forced to take on caregiving responsibilities at home, and Cariloop was there to help them. It has received accolades from communities in several states, and it raised $15 million in Series B funding in 2021, to hire more people with the goal of tripling the size of the business. Michael believes there's never been a time when it was needed so much.

ATLANTA: The A-Town

When we scheduled a Rise of the Rest tour for Atlanta in 2015, I reached out to an Atlanta native, Ross Baird, who had founded Village Capital, a DC-based impact investment fund I had backed when it was getting started. Ross acknowledged that as much as he loved his hometown, he'd never found Atlanta to be particularly welcoming to entrepreneurs, which is why he left and moved to DC. The focus, he said, had been on the big Fortune 500 companies based there, such as Delta Airlines, Coca-Cola, Home Depot, and UPS, causing investors to be somewhat risk-averse and disinclined to invest in entrepreneurs.

But that was already starting to change. These large anchor corporations were beginning to collaborate with universities and local communities to create innovation centers. They were ready to put skin in the game because they saw the advantage to their own businesses of promoting startups. Large companies, including AT&T, Chick-fil-A, Cox Enterprises, Delta Air Lines, Georgia-Pacific, Georgia Power Foundation, Intercontinental Exchange, Invesco, Home Depot, and UPS collaborated with Georgia Tech and Tech Square Ventures to launch Engage, a venture fund and accelerator.

The city was stepping up as well. On our Rise of the Rest tour we visited Georgia Tech's Advanced Technology Development Center, which was emerging as an important accelerator,

and Ponce City Market, a groundbreaking real estate development by local firm Jamestown. Jim Irwin, the lead on the project, explained, "We want to be where startups go to grow." We
visited a variety of companies, including the marketing platform Mailchimp, which had struggled to raise venture capital
when it got started in 2001, as few investors were willing to back
Atlanta startups back then. That proved to be a miscall, as in
2021 Mailchimp was acquired for $12 billion—a stunning out-
come for an Atlanta startup, and a sign that Atlanta was indeed
on the rise.

After we left Mailchimp and Ponce City Market, we traveled
across town to visit Opportunity Hub, a platform for Black entrepreneurs. Its founder Rodney Sampson has an interesting
backstory. He was studying for his MBA at the Keller Graduate
School of Management and working as the chief administrator
at Mount Carmel Baptist Church in Atlanta when he had an
epiphany. The church's pastor, Timothy Flemming, had gained
a wide audience for his popular sermons, but it was costing him
a lot of money every month to buy cable TV time to air them.
Rodney thought he saw a better way—harnessing streaming
technology to deliver sermons to a worldwide audience, not just
for Pastor Flemming but for others as well. With two partners
from Georgia Tech, Rodney launched Streamingfaith.com, the
first internet live-streaming network for churches and faith-
based content.

For Rodney, it was an early trial by fire in the world of raising venture capital as a young Black man. He succeeded, later
selling Streamingfaith.com to a media company for nearly $20
million. And from that point on, his life's work was laid out for
him.

As an early Black tech startup founder, Rodney quickly realized that he was facing an uphill battle. But Rodney's faith in the potential of Black entrepreneurs was unwavering. He became an organizer, mentor, and evangelist, linking the civil rights legacy to entrepreneurship. Martin Luther King Jr. was "entrepreneurial in spirit," Rodney wrote in his 2012 book, *Kingonomics*. "He had the drive, innovation and risk-taking nature of an entrepreneur. He also deeply understood the value of collaboration, not just as a social tool but as a business principle." The success of the book led to a thriving Kingonomics conference program and set the stage for Rodney's next innovation.

In 2013, Rodney and his wife Shanterria took their commitment a big step forward. On the fiftieth anniversary of the March on Washington for Jobs and Freedom, they launched Opportunity Hub. OHUB became the first multicampus Black-owned coworking space, entrepreneurship center, and tech hub. It isn't just a place for entrepreneurs and budding startups to gather. OHUB provides a rich array of services and support. It's a startup pre-accelerator, a coding boot camp, a scholarship initiative, and an angel investing platform for underserved communities, reducing the barriers Black founders face. Its entrepreneurial curriculum features over three hundred events a year. In 2015 Rodney launched a second Opportunity Hub property, Tech-Square Labs, on the west side of Atlanta near Georgia Tech.

I felt I could relate to Rodney, because we were both trying to end the cycle of money flowing to the same kinds of people, in the same places, for the same ideas. That meant making sure that a broad and diverse group of founders from across the nation had seats at the venture table.

The winners of the Atlanta pitch competition were Black cofounders Jewel Burks and Jason Crain, who had started their company, PartPic, while working for a vehicle repair company.

PartPic allowed repair professionals to save time and money by offering technology that identified key parts via smartphone photos.

A year after our tour Rodney wrote a powerful piece about our common goals: "Throughout history, allies have been re-quired for equity, parity and opportunity to occur for Black people in America: In the 1800s, it was the abolitionists and legal community. In the 1900s, it was the politicians, govern-ment agencies and large corporations." Now, in the twenty-first century, he wrote, the leading allies would be a mixture of supportive entrepreneurs and patrons, popular cultural icons that put a spotlight on Black innovators, and research-driven institutions such as Georgia Tech and Morehouse College of Medicine, which had championed innovation in the commu-nity. "It's the organized intersection of innovation, culture and capital that will position America to take advantage of the op-portunity it has to fulfill the promises made at the inception of this country, and ensure that all its citizens can participate in what we call the new opportunity economy."

A Young Founder Breaks Through

Sean Henry was only eighteen when he launched Stord. But he first dipped his toe in the world of e-commerce and sup-ply chains in elementary school, buying broken computers and phones on Craigslist, fixing them, and selling them for parts or as reconstructed items on eBay. So, while still a child, Sean was learning about the tough world of logistics. "I got very used to shipping inventory and always had challenges around parcel rates and costs, eating into my overall margins while guaran-teeing good delivery to my end customers." In high school he developed a similar business, focusing on specialty automotive parts. He procured brake pads, exhaust parts, and more, and then sold them on a small e-commerce store. Everything about it was challenging. It was hard to get competitive shipping rates and to stock inventory in his parents' garage. These difficulties eventually became the genesis of Stord. Smaller suppliers could not achieve the fulfillment and shipping advantage against big companies like Walmart and Amazon. Sean wanted to create a platform and the software that would give them that advantage.

When he started, Sean had to build relationships with potential investors from scratch. When he pitched Stord, they invariably asked him, "Why are you in Atlanta?" People would say, "You should move today." Potential investors were especially eager to see Stord on the West Coast, where it could benefit from all Silicon Valley had to offer. But Sean stuck to his guns. "For me, it comes down to the fact that there are enterprise customers here that aren't in the Bay Area," he said. "Atlanta is a hub for Fortune 500 companies."

In particular, Sean found the talent pool in Atlanta to be stronger and more stable. In Silicon Valley, talent tended to jump to the next big thing. "The talent here is very mission driven. They want to be at companies for a long time and build them into something very successful."

Sean also noted a piece of conventional wisdom that seems to hold true: "It's often a lot easier to build a company when you're either a medium-sized fish or big fish in a smaller or medium-sized pond." As a case in point, he cited the immense support Stord has received from Georgia Tech, from the Metro Atlanta Chamber of Commerce, and from all corners of the ecosystem. "They send us talent, they send us customers, they invite us to events, they introduce us to investors," he said. This collaborative environment is a dramatic departure from the cutthroat norm, and Sean credits the culture of Atlanta.

With this support, Stord has grown in seven years to a billion-dollar unicorn company, thanks to a $90 million round in 2021 led by legendary Silicon Valley VC firm Kleiner Perkins— another big win for the Atlanta startup community.

That may be a reason to celebrate, but there were some challenges, especially around the pandemic. "Because demand was so high there were capacity crunches," Sean said. "It was hard to get trucks. It was hard to hire workers. There was a driver shortage. There was a chassis shortage. So it's been a very challenging two years in supply chains, but Stord is an agile logistics network. Meaning our whole network approach lets you use any of our warehouses very flexibly on our platform versus piecing together leases or long-term contracts." He has seen companies come around to the idea that they have to be more agile too, and that's good for his business.

"We use the word *democratizing* a lot internally because we're democratizing access to all the great logistics of volume out there for all these warehouses who couldn't access it," he told us. It's a simple goal, and it's working. Stord could very well be Atlanta's next Fortune 500 company.

DENVER: Mile-High Opportunity

My father, Daniel Case, studied law at the University of Denver before returning home to practice in Hawaii. He spoke of the physical beauty of Colorado, but in the 1940s Denver's promise was not especially evident, as its economy was too reliant on a few sectors such as oil and gas. Today the city has flourished and is now at or near the top of every "desirable city" ranking you can find. It is the number one relocation destination in the United States for skilled workers ages twenty-five to forty-four.

Not only does Denver offer a great lifestyle, stunning geography, and beautiful weather (we were told it boasts three hundred days of sunshine a year) but its business environment for startups is exceptional. The welcome sign is out. According to the Kauffman Foundation, Denver is one of the top five cities in terms of startup activity, and Colorado ranks number four in the nation. When Rise of the Rest visited the city in 2016, we saw every sign of that. First to impress us was the obvious commitment of local and state officials. Then-governor (and former entrepreneur) John Hickenlooper, who is now a US senator, joined our tour to talk about all the ways Colorado was supporting entrepreneurs. Mayor Michael Hancock, Denver's second Black mayor, was equally bullish on business development, and startups in particular. Mayor Hancock told us that in a five-year period over five thousand companies had started or relocated in Denver. It's interesting that Denver is something of a hub for startups founded by military veterans, such as Techstars offshoot Patriot Boot Camp, which equips military members, veterans, and their families with the tools to become successful entrepreneurs.

With ten Fortune 500 companies and an engaged university system, the entrepreneurial ecosystem has flourished in Denver. One stop on our tour was the Turing School of Software and Design, which is generating a continuous talent pool for the area's startups.

During our roundtable later in the day, we asked several startup founders to tell us why Denver was such an appealing place to do business, and every one of them mentioned quality of life, followed by a culture of caring and community. Many cited the leadership of entrepreneurs such as Brad Feld, a founder of Techstars and pioneer in building startup communities, and entrepreneurs-turned-politicians like Jared Polis, who after great success as an internet entrepreneur pivoted to politics and at the time of our visit was serving in Congress, where he was a champion for entrepreneurs. (Jared was later elected governor of Colorado in 2018 and would continue prioritizing entrepreneurs.) It was clear that Denver had great momentum, but many were unaware. I urged the founders to find a way to spread the word. "Denver has already risen," I said. "It just needs a way to tell its story."

A Founder's Motto: Give and Receive

Erik Mitisek is a veteran of Startup Colorado, from the Startup America Partnership, and he calls himself a career ecosystem builder—a founder of Denver Startup Week, among other initiatives. I first met Erik in 2002 when I invested in Denver-based Exclusive Resorts, one of the first "sharing economy" companies, where he was a key executive. He then spent much of a decade focused on building the Colorado startup ecosystem, including serving as chief innovation officer for Governor Hickenlooper. Now, with his startup Highwing, an insurance tech company, Erik seeks to streamline a very old industry.

"Our north star is to save time in the procurement of insurance," he said, noting that a client told him that on average it takes forty-four days from the first contact to the writing of the policy. "There are a lot of things that can be built in forty-four days. So, there's a path to save time by as much as twenty percent and streamline the business in the process."

It might be a worthwhile endeavor, but the barriers to taking on the insurance industry are unusually high. "We're building a company in a field where nothing is really broken," Erik admitted. "The system works, even though it may be inefficient." And it works at such an enormous scale that it's hard for disrupters to land a punch. "These are challenges we work on every day," Erik said.

His close engagement in the Denver tech community has been invaluable. "The biggest takeaway for me is that you get back what you put in. And so, as I was building Highwing, I had endless founders and partners and friends either make investment introductions or talent introductions. The community has really embraced the business."

Erik believes this is part of the "give first" mentality that anchors those in the startup community. "The more that you give, the more that you get back. And it's not a one for one trade. It's a belief that if you're generous, generosity will cycle back. The ecosystem relationships are rocket ships and I feel like the relationships through things like the Startup America Partnership and the Rise of the Rest have connected not just the entrepreneurs to Denver, but Denver to the world."

Those ecosystem relationships were in evidence during the pandemic, which tested the mettle of the community. "Entrepreneurs are built to be adaptive," Erik observed. "You wake up every single day and your number one mode in life is adaptation. And so I looked at the pandemic as a huge opportunity."

What others might have found disorienting, Erik took as a fascinating challenge and a chance to poke at the future. "It's been a huge opportunity to learn how to be a leader in a remote environment," he said. "It's an entirely different skillset to work in an asynchronous world versus a synchronous world. It was an entrepreneurial challenge that I was really excited about. And I thought it was an opportunity for our business."

The bottom line: "I've always been a person who has asked the question when I wake up: how can I be useful? I ask it in my marriage. I ask it in my child's life. I ask it as a founder and leader of a company. And most importantly, I ask it in the community that I live in. I get a tremendous amount of energy from giving back and from being useful in the community. And I try to find other entrepreneurs and leaders that have that quality and amplify it. At its core, ecosystem building is being useful to your community. Those who embrace that are going to rise in their communities to be the ones that drive success."

SEVEN

The Revival of Iconic Regions

What's it going to take to bring struggling regions of the country back—to demonstrate to their citizens that they are not forgotten or left behind? Many of these iconic regions were vital to the life and growth of America before falling behind in the new economy. But a revival is happening, led by the entrepreneurial community, and a growing number of entrepreneurs are hearing the call of home.

The coasts have long been draws for young, ambitious people with dreams of making it in places where success seemed to have a greater cache. But when entrepreneurs see a chance to thrive in their own communities, many of them rethink the advantage of leaving home. "They're willing to be inspired by their community," John Lettieri, president and CEO of the Economic Innovation Group (a DC think tank focused on geographic inequality), observes. "What is always striking is how loyal people are to their communities." When that loyalty pays off in the chance to prosper and do groundbreaking work in their industries, it's a win-win.

CENTRAL PENNSYLVANIA: Harnessing American History

The spirit of America, reflected in its long history of innovation, brought Rise of the Rest to central Pennsylvania in October 2017—specifically to the cluster of small cities of Harrisburg, Lancaster, and York. Each of these cities is around fifty thousand people, barely a blip on the map in one respect. Normally, they'd have little chance of competing on their own, as a robust tech ecosystem. However, it's intriguing to consider how a cluster of small cities located in a sweet spot, with Philadelphia to the east and Pittsburgh to the west, and equidistant from New York City and Washington, DC, could potentially become a seat of opportunity and a magnet for capital.

For those who might doubt the ability of little guys like these to compete, there's a riveting example in this bucolic landscape—the story of the York Plan. It's the kind of thing that instantly captures one's imagination, a heroic World War II effort that to this day its residents proudly herald as a decisive step in the Allied victory.

The York Plan was an agreement among industries to work together in a unique collaboration. Early in the war, leaders at the Manufacturers Association of York realized that their industries were too small to compete for military contracts. So, they devised a plan to pool their efforts, sharing workers and machinery across the board. Their fifteen-point plan was designed to use every resource available—"to get idle tools and idle men working."

The U.S. government was so impressed with the York Plan that it promoted it as a model for other communities and even produced a wartime movie about it. A mural, "York Goes to War," is painted on the south wall of the Bell Socialization Services building in the heart of town.

After the war, York shifted gears, and the York Plan became a model for a manufacturing boom in the area. Producing everything from refrigeration machinery to the popular candy York Peppermint Patties, its success brought large companies to the area, including Caterpillar and Continental Wire and Cable. In recent decades, however, the area suffered a manufacturing decline.

Undaunted, York and some visionary entrepreneurs worked on ways to revive opportunities. "We changed the world then," Kevin Schreiber, president and CEO of the York County Economic Alliance, wrote in his pitch to bring Rise of the Rest to town. "York can lead by example to reshape our American economy by creating a York Plan for the 21st Century that redefines the relationship between industry, innovation, community and entrepreneurship."

York was certainly enthusiastic—our Rise of the Rest bus was greeted by a marching band. The pitch competition was sold out, and the winner, the startup Device Events, a subscription service that helps medical providers identify problems with medical devices, marked a sign of the times—a pivot from distressed industries to thriving concepts like health care technology.

We also met a local entrepreneur named John McElligott. McElligott is a student of York history and passionate about the rise of smaller US cities. He moved to York from Baltimore a decade ago because he was attracted to its strong sense of community. He vowed to replace lost manufacturing jobs and put York on the cutting edge.

In 2015, McElligott launched York Exponential, a robotics startup that lets manufacturers lease collaborative robots by the hour. In 2017, he added the Fortress Initiative, a nonprofit that manages a coding and robotics boot camp. On our tour a local student, trained at the boot camp, helped me program a robot.

McElligott aims to make York the center of robotics innovation—as he put it, "a beacon" to other communities. He likes to point out that the original York Plan's fifteen-point outline "included terms and models Silicon Valley thought it invented a decade ago—crowdfunding, crowdsourcing, makerspaces, and a resource sharing economy."

In the year after we visited York, McElligott realized his goal of establishing the York Plan 2.0 Innovation District, a tech project approved for a $6 million grant from Pennsylvania's Redevelopment Assistance Capital Program. The York Innovation District is now a partially completed redevelopment of two acres in the city of York's Northwest Triangle. The design is a ten-story, 240,000-square-foot facility that will include space for robotics manufacturing, robotics research, laboratories, and prototyping.

In addition to the robotics-focused building, the plan includes a mixed-use development, with residential living, retail space, and about 140 parking spots. There will also be an amenity area with a fitness center, bike center, coworking space, and other game areas.

York has an ecosystem made up of the Fortress Academy, an incubator; the York city government, the Commonwealth of Pennsylvania, and the York City Redevelopment Authority, representing local government; York Exponential, as a tentpole company; and the *York Dispatch*, as local media. And it's not just entrepreneurs who are finding York a great place to live. Jeff Koons, one of America's most famous artists, grew up in York and never left. He spends time in the other, better known,

York—New York City—but has never abandoned his hometown for what many might have considered greener pastures.

Jared Isaacman, who led the first all-civilian space flight in 2021, also shares a passion for Pennsylvania. He started and scaled Shift4 in Allentown, and its success as a payment processor turned Jared into a billionaire. Jared still leads Shift4, but his passion from an early age was space. He sponsored the SpaceX flight and used it as a platform to raise money for charity, raising almost $250 million for St. Jude's Hospital. Many followed Jared's SpaceX flight with interest, and most probably heard he was a successful entrepreneur. Few might have appreciated that his success was in the city of Allentown, which Billy Joel once sang about having closed all the factories down.

Central Pennsylvania has a ways to go toward revival, but it seems to me that York is a model of what it could become. The energy of this place is not surprising given its connection to the origins of our nation. To travel through Pennsylvania is to be constantly reminded of the country's founding, and York is a shining example. Between September 1777 and June 1778, the Continental Congress, which was engaged in writing a blueprint for the emerging nation, was forced to move the government from Philadelphia to York to protect itself from the advancing British army. Huddled together in the courthouse on the square, our nation's founders set aside disputes to adopt the Articles of Confederation and Perpetual Union, which would bring the United States into being. This early act of collaboration—and creation—is often on the minds of people in the area who strive to build a new era of opportunity.

I always remind entrepreneurs, in the spirit of our nation's founders, that entrepreneurship is hard. Entrepreneurs are surrounded by doubters and skeptics—even including family and friends who are acting out of love. To press on, through doubt and fear, with no certainty of what will come—that's the courage it takes to ultimately prevail.

PITTSBURGH: From Steeltown to Techtown

Pittsburgh is often cited as one of the most promising comeback cities, thanks to a strong technology bent. There were plenty of naysayers about the Steel City transitioning into a tech-forward city. It had to face high barriers to begin to break through—the first being overcoming the pejorative label of being in the "rust belt." People often use that term without thinking about what it means—that the cities that powered the Industrial Revolution and built America are now *rusted*. If you're living there it's a slap in the face that diminishes your past and suggests that you have no future. Psychologically, that attitude drives the divisions between old and new. But it also gets under the skin of some entrepreneurs, who set out to prove the skeptics wrong.

Rise of the Rest included Pittsburgh in our first tour because it was an iconic city that, just like Detroit, built America. At its high point, it produced most of the world's steel. Then, like the rest of the manufacturing sector, the city suffered, as new technologies and globalization began to impact manufacturing jobs. But Pittsburgh had a clear path to the future, thanks to the choices made by one of its immigrant fathers, Andrew Carnegie.

Andrew Carnegie emigrated with his family from Scotland in 1848 and settled in Pittsburgh. As a young teenager he got a job in a textile mill working as a "bobbin boy," changing spools of thread. Through a combination of natural talent, voracious curiosity, and independent business sense, he got an education and rose up to build the largest steel production company in the world. He also had a philanthropic instinct and once said that "to die rich is to die disgraced." In 1900, Carnegie donated $1 million (over $33 million in today's dollars) to build a technical institute in Pittsburgh where ordinary working-class people could learn trades and improve their skills. The Carnegie Technical School quickly developed into something more—a well-rounded baccalaureate program that included colleges of engineering and the arts, as well as a college for women.

Carnegie died in 1919, but his legacy lived on, in large part through Carnegie Tech. In 1967 the college merged with another prominent Pittsburgh family institution, the Mellon Institute of science and research, becoming Carnegie Mellon University. Then in 1979 the university made a fortuitous decision, forming the Robotics Institute just when robotics was gaining a foothold in the manufacturing sector.

When robots first started showing up on the factory floor, there was deep fear and resentment among American workers. The prospect of being replaced by robots was not just a science fiction nightmare but a looming reality, especially as jobs in manufacturing were in steady decline.

Ironically, robotics in Pittsburgh became an example of the adage preached by the likes of Henry Ford and others that success comes to those who embrace their fears. Today, Pittsburgh is vying to become the robotics capital of the world.

Carnegie Mellon has attracted some of the best and brightest STEM students, but for a long time the graduates didn't stay in Pittsburgh, often heading for Silicon Valley or Boston when they left school. Acknowledging this brain drain, community, business, and educational leaders knew they had to find a way to create a more robust economic foundation. That included developing more of a startup ecosystem.

Today, more people graduating from Carnegie Mellon are staying in Pittsburgh. Some join startups; others join big companies like Facebook and Google that have offices there, each with hundreds of employees.

On our tour we held events at Carnegie Mellon, including a session around robotics. Robotics is more than just the arms and legs of the Terminator, as one of my colleagues put it. It's the artificial intelligence engine. AI has driven new technologies like Duolingo, a wildly successful language learning program and app, which started as a Carnegie Mellon project in 2009 by Professor Luis von Ahn and his postgraduate student Severin Hacker. Both immigrants—from Guatemala and Switzerland, respectively—they knew how challenging and expensive it can be to learn a new language. Duolingo was designed as a free program, supported by advertising. It took off—Ashton Kutcher was an early investor. The iPhone app was released in 2012 and the Android version in 2013. It currently has over 300 million registered users and went public in 2021, at a $4 billion valuation—a visible sign of what's possible in Pittsburgh.

Duolingo has constantly evolved over its history, and its founders recognized that Pittsburgh was the ideal setting for growth, with its wealth of AI talent. And that's how ecosystems get built.

I marveled at the rapidly developing Pittsburgh ecosystem, so much of it engineered by Carnegie Mellon. I mentioned to then-president of CMU Subra Suresh that people didn't always know Pittsburgh's tech story because the locals didn't like to brag about themselves. But the numbers are impressive."

President Suresh told me that Carnegie Mellon was now in the top five US universities attracting venture capital in companies started by grads—with the other four on the coasts. It was notable that seven out of the ten Pittsburgh pitch competition finalists on our tour had links to Carnegie Mellon, as did the winner, SolePower, a shoe insole that stores energy created when walking or running in a battery that can be used to charge electronic devices such as cellphones or tablets.

Founders Hahna Alexander and Matthew Stanton, College of Engineering graduates, got plenty of help along the way from the CMU startup ecosystem. As such, the idea had a well-established foundation, with support from CMU's Open Field Entrepreneurs Fund, the Center for Innovation and Entrepreneurship, and the Center for Technology Transfer and Enterprise Creation. We were intrigued by the creative use of technology, and encouraged by the interest SolePower was generating from the Department of Defense and outdoor gear companies. The celebrated Pittsburgh Steeler Franco Harris, who was a pitch competition judge, observed that although he didn't do much running anymore, he was still impressed with the concept of using natural movement to power technology. (As a regretful aside, I'll note that SolePower, despite a strong start, didn't survive the seed stage—a reminder that even the best ideas can fall by the wayside in the intense startup arena.)

Pittsburgh's status as an emerging tech center was reinforced by a 2017 Brookings report titled "Capturing the Next Economy: Pittsburgh's Rise as a Global Innovation City." The report noted: "Few cities have experienced the economic upheaval that Pittsburgh did in the 1970s and 1980s—and come back. During the country's industrial heyday, the city swelled in population and income. Yet by 1980, global economic forces had shuttered much of the U.S. steel industry, and Pittsburgh's unemployment rate reached 18 percent as Western Pennsylvania effectively experienced a second Great Depression. Today, the competitive advantage of the region is no longer its rivers and raw materials but its high-skilled workers, world-class research institutions, and technology-intense advanced manufacturing."

In particular, the Brookings report highlighted Pittsburgh's Oakland neighborhood, home to Carnegie Mellon University, the University of Pittsburgh, and the University of Pittsburgh Medical Center, as well as dozens of startups and coworking spaces. Pittsburgh is poised to become a great tech city. What's needed now, says Brookings's Mark Muro, is a comprehensive and bold effort to turbocharge growth.

OMAHA: Gateway to Promise

Middle America has been feeling anxious for a long time, and I can understand that. While the heartland struggles to keep its industries and communities relevant, it is bombarded with news from what seems like another planet, with stories about robots and driverless cars and space tourism and disruption. People feel left out and left behind because none of those futuristic conversations seem to have anything to do with their reality.

What the disenfranchised can't yet see is that a vibrant technological future is possible in their own backyards; they just need a way to usher it in. It's easy to forget that the greatest inventions in our history were figured out in someone's garage or barn or school lab—the most common settings. That spirit of invention doesn't belong to the coasts. In every case, someone had to take a chance on a new idea, support it, invest in it. Until recently, that investment has been lacking in middle America.

"*Never* bet against America." The admonition came from none other than Warren Buffett in his 2021 shareholder letter. Known as the Oracle of Omaha, Warren has been distinguished not only by his financial genius but by his hometown Omaha roots. He has spent only a handful of his ninety years outside of Nebraska and explains that it's where he can think clearly away from the distracting noise. I've always found many reasons to admire Warren—his humility, his philanthropic instincts, and his brilliance. Above all that, he speaks with moving conviction about his love for middle America. In his 2021 letter to shareholders, he spent some time describing his state's history and extolling its glorious past.

"Today, with much of finance, media, government and technology located in coastal areas, it's easy to overlook the many miracles occurring in middle America," he wrote. He related one local example that was especially close to his heart, the story of Nebraska Furniture Mart. Its founder, Rose Blumkin, "Mrs. B," was a Russian immigrant who first arrived in Seattle in 1915, unable to speak or read English. A few years later she moved to Omaha, where she scraped together enough money to start a furniture store.

Mrs. B struggled, and World War II made things worse. She closed 1946 with only meager earnings. "One invaluable asset, however, went unrecorded in the 1946 figures," Warren wrote. "Louie Blumkin, Mrs. B's only son, had rejoined the store after four years in the U.S. Army. Louie fought at Normandy's

Omaha Beach following the D-Day invasion, earned a Purple Heart for injuries sustained in the Battle of the Bulge, and finally sailed home in November 1945. Once Mrs. B and Louie were reunited, there was no stopping Nebraska Furniture Mart. Driven by their dream, mother and son worked days, nights, and weekends. The result was a retailing miracle."

In 1983, with the company then worth $60 million, Warren made a handshake purchase of 80 percent of the business. Mrs. B. and her family would continue to run it, and she went to work every day until she was 103.

"A post-script to this story says it all," Warren wrote. "When Mrs. B's large family gathered for holiday meals, she always asked that they sing a song before eating. Her selection never varied: Irving Berlin's 'God Bless America.'"

He went on to celebrate that spirit in the country: "Success stories abound throughout America. Since our country's birth, individuals with an idea, ambition and often just a pittance of capital have succeeded beyond their dreams by creating something new or by improving the customer's experience with something old."

Warren has a gift for speaking plain truths, and his shareholder letters are known for that. His success has come from buying large, established, profitable companies with strong competitive moats, and he's never been comfortable investing in startups. But he recognizes their importance. We had dinner the night before we kicked off our Rise of the Rest bus tour in Omaha, and discussed the fact that Omaha needed a next act, as all of its Fortune 500 companies had started more than a century ago. Warren was grateful that we were taking the lead in seeding startups and hoped some would rise to lead Omaha's next chapter.

The influence of another mover, Jeff Raikes, pervades the entrepreneur culture of Omaha. Jeff's story also speaks to the powerful draw of the hometown. Growing up on his family's farm in Ashland, thirty minutes from Omaha, he was immersed in farm life. Before he was ten Jeff had mastered the tractor and was working in the cornfields. He always figured he'd pursue a career in something ag related, and he went to Stanford with a plan to get a degree in agricultural policy. But then his life took a turn. Silicon Valley called to him, and when he graduated, he went to work for Steve Jobs at his fledgling company, Apple Computer. After a couple of years, Jeff left Apple to join Bill Gates at Microsoft in Seattle, and that's where he stayed for twenty-eight years, rising to various leadership roles before being named president in 2005. He later became CEO of the Bill & Melinda Gates Foundation and is currently the chair of Stanford University. With his own foundation, Jeff is a great benefactor for the startup ecosystem in Nebraska, and a strong supporter of the University of Nebraska–Lincoln Jeffrey S. Raikes School of Computer Science and Management.

Nebraska is an example of how a phenomenal university system can help grow a tech ecosystem. In addition to Jeff's effort, the University of Nebraska–Lincoln Innovation Campus will facilitate connections with the private sector. It is expected that over five thousand people will work on the 2.2 million-square-foot campus.

A key theme that comes up in places like Omaha and nearby Lincoln is the bridge between a glorious past driven by legacy industries and corporations, and an open future where the script is still being written. Many of these sectors of the economy have been outsourced or moved, and many legacy companies have also moved, shut down, or been diminished. How do they build and tell the story of the community's resurgence? Some look to the past for inspiration.

In 1863, in the midst of the Civil War, construction began on the first transcontinental railroad, creating a line of transit between Omaha and Sacramento. It was such a momentous point in history that Rise of the Rest started its Omaha 2016 tour at Lauritzen Gardens, the original demarcation point. We acknowledged the boldness of the transcontinental venture. Not only was the nation at war but the West was still unsettled and treacherous. What made the difference was the 1800s version of a startup ecosystem—companies, local officials, the federal government, investors, and activists who demanded that the nation rise above the despair evoked by war to carve out a promising future in the rugged terrain. Omaha was the gateway to that promise. But like many heartland communities, it has confronted serious economic headwinds in the twenty-first century.

One of the early challenges faced by the tech startup ecosystem in Lincoln and Omaha was a lack of capital. It's not that money wasn't there. There are enough legacy businesses in Omaha to create a substantial support system. But, like Warren Buffett, many of them choose to invest in established sectors, like public stocks or real estate, not startups.

The startup community was in part rescued by the formation of Nebraska Angels in 2006. The Angels are a network with a mission to build the entrepreneurial community by connecting entrepreneurs with investors. At the time of our visit, they had made over sixty venture investments, totaling around $120 million. While we were in Lincoln, we visited one of the startup stars everyone was talking about—sports technology company Hudl, with its video analytics software that helps teams maximize performance. Hudl had just raised a $72.5 million Series C funding round—massive for Lincoln.

One of the aims of our Nebraska tour was to encourage the idea of forming a regional ecosystem, with Lincoln and Omaha, which are only about an hour away from each other. To push that strategy, we drove founders on the bus between the two cities as a way of connecting and saying, "Hey, the drive is not that far." Even though they lived only an hour apart, most of them had never met one another. But they were certainly willing. Time and again on the tour we heard people mention Nebraska's welcoming spirit, sometimes dubbed "Nebraska nice." As one of the participants on the tour emphasized, "This region has strong community support, an open-door environment. Almost anyone is willing to sit down and have a coffee to talk through an idea."

An Omaha Startup's Family Values

The winner of the Nebraska Rise of the Rest pitch competition was LifeLoop, an app-based connection service for families with elder adults in care facilities and assisted living. The founder of LifeLoop, Amy Johnson, who graduated from the University of Nebraska–Lincoln with a degree in human resources and family science, had never aspired to be an entrepreneur. After a number of years working in various capacities for Mutual of Omaha, she took a job running sales and marketing for her father-in-law, an entrepreneur who had started an insurance company. She was starting to feel restless, wanting a new challenge when one presented itself.

Amy's husband Kent's elderly grandmother had been placed in a memory care facility, and the family was struggling to keep track of what was happening to her. The worst problem was the lack of communication. Amy's father-in-law, the primary advocate, would show up and be given a surprise laundry list of issues, and a demand to pay for more services, without a coherent explanation of why his mother's needs had changed. He wanted to do right by his mother, but he felt out of the loop. "We always felt like it was very reactive," Amy said. "We'd go to call her, and she wouldn't answer, so we'd call the front desk, and there had been a shift change. Nobody had a way to know what happened that day, to accurately communicate it to us. That just created a lot of assumptions. Assumptions are usually not great because you make up a scenario in your head that you're then believing." There was also a quality-of-life issue in finding ways to engage grandma with her community and with family across the country.

Amy and Kent, a commodities trader, knew nothing about the senior living industry, but they strongly believed there had to be a better way. Along with their friend Phil, a lawyer, they began doing research about creating an app that would help keep families connected while providing a needed backup for staff. The simple idea started with the thought, "There has to be a better way."

It was a grueling process of trial and error. "We were so naive," Amy said, describing those early days. "None of us knew how to build software. Now we do. None of us were from senior living. We just started saying, 'Okay, what step needs to happen first?' At that point, we engaged with a freelancer, and it did not go well. Not because of them. We had no idea what we were doing. Then we found a software company based in Omaha, called Aviture. They do a lot of government contracts, but those contracts come in waves. During the downtime, they wanted other projects to work on in what they called the Garage. They took us on and were a huge part of us getting off the ground with that initial product."

The app is simple to use and comprehensive, with full communications and record-keeping functions. It allows residents to quickly communicate, access their calendars, chat with family members, share pictures and videos, arrange transportation, and enable staff to track residents' needs and progress. They formalized LifeLoop in January 2015 and Amy quit her job so she could step in full-time as CEO.

The first year was a struggle. The early adopters were their bread and butter and saw them through. Amy built new customer buy-in through empathy and humility. "A big part of it was relationship building—and taking ego out of the process. I made it clear that it wasn't about me and what I was building, it was about them and what they needed—and how I could best support them."

Meanwhile, Amy was becoming involved in Omaha's fledgling tech ecosystem, and finding professional support there. When Rise of the Rest was planning its 2016 tour, she got a call from Jeff Slobotski, the founder of Silicon Prairie News and the host of the Big Omaha startup conference, who encouraged her to enter the pitch competition. An early leader of the startup scene in Omaha, Jeff has become a figurehead for entrepreneurs, and when he makes a call, people tend to listen. Amy agreed to enter the competition.

"I was a nervous wreck because it was in front of two thousand people," she recalled. But her supporters kept saying, "Just be yourself. You know this." And she got up and gave an engaging and persuasive presentation. We thought LifeLoop had a lot of promise, and we gave Amy the check.

Winning the Rise of the Rest competition was a big confidence booster, and it also opened more doors. The next years were spent building the brand and engaging more communities and family members. LifeLoop grew rapidly. It's now found in over seven hundred retirement communities in forty states and is just one example of how entrepreneurs are nimbly responding to changing demographics by creating breakthrough industries such as health care technology.

When the pandemic hit, overnight the nation's attention was turned toward senior living centers, where the danger was most grave. Under lockdown, just communicating was often impossible. LifeLoop was the right product for the times, a literal lifesaver. "It went from a nice-to-have product to a must-have product," Amy said. Their numbers skyrocketed during the pandemic.

When things opened up, and Amy was able to travel again, she discovered just how needed LifeLoop was. She was on a Southwest flight coming home from Portland, and she was exhausted. She just wanted to put her headphones on and listen to a podcast and fall asleep. Two ladies were sitting next to her in the middle and window seats, and much to Amy's chagrin, one of them started talking to her, asking what she did for a living.

"I sell software," Amy replied. It was her go-to answer when she didn't want to talk. And then, to be polite, she asked, "What do you do for a living?" The woman said, "I work in senior living."

Amy sat up straighter. "Actually, here is my company," she said, showing the woman the app.

"LifeLoop!" she said enthusiastically. "I use it every single day."

"So do I," the second woman chimed in. It turned out she had a family member in a senior living center and that's how they communicated.

Amy no longer felt exhausted. She was exhilarated by the simple reminder of the impact her work was having for ordinary people.

In March 2022, LifeLoop merged with iN2L, a Vista Equity portfolio company and leading provider of digital engagement to the senior living market. Amy will serve as chief strategy officer of the expanded venture.

EIGHT

Live-Work-Play

The last big real estate movement occurred after World War II, when millions of returning soldiers catalyzed a change in where and how Americans worked and lived. The resulting development of large downtown office buildings and suburban commuter communities set in place a lifestyle pattern that continued largely unchanged for the next two generations. It could be characterized as SLEEP-COMMUTE-WORK-COMMUTE-SLEEP. Now, because of tech-driven cultural and work shifts, post-pandemic trends, and the preferences of millennials and other younger workers, communities are reconfiguring in a model of LIVE-WORK-PLAY. The emphasis is on livability.

The tech industry was long notorious for its high-stress work culture. Companies in Silicon Valley often provided catered meals, laundry services, and chair massages, as they wanted to create a comfortable and stress-free environment, but also because many of their employees worked very long hours. Unfortunately, sometimes this went too far, and the combination of an intense focus on productivity and a win-at-all-costs culture created a male-centric workforce, defined by the popular slang as "tech bros."

Thankfully, the times are changing. Today's top talent is attracted not only to what's happening inside the company but also to the lifestyle on the outside.

SALT LAKE CITY: Silicon Slopes

Salt Lake City is a blend of an appealing outdoors-centric city and a culture of giving back that infuses the startup community. Historically, it has stayed mostly under the radar in conversations about business and startups, but that's changing quickly. To the outside world it's often known for its stunning mountains, or for the family culture, grounded in the Church of Jesus Christ of Latter-day Saints (LDS). For these reasons, it comes as a surprise for many to learn that Salt Lake City is one of the leading beneficiaries of venture capital and is increasingly referred to in the startup world as "the Silicon slopes."

Fraser Nelson, former director of strategic partnership at Sorenson Impact, a leading impact investor, wrote about the city's unique startup culture for our Rise of the Rest playbook. "When I moved to Utah 20 years ago, my friends on the East and West Coasts knew the state for one thing—the greatest snow on earth," she wrote. "What they and the rest of the country are finally coming to realize is that Utah offers an entrepreneur's playground. My office at Sorenson Impact on the University of Utah campus is a block from the Lassonde Entrepreneur Institute, just one of the reasons the 'U' is rated the No. 1 School for Entrepreneurs by LendEDU." The reason, she suggests, is a blend of serious commitment by business and government with a strong sense of community engagement.

A big driver of entrepreneurship there is a culture of giving back and doing good, and there is a strong pay-it-forward attitude in the community that is reflected in many of the startup models.

Fraser makes the point that it's not all about the money in Salt Lake: "Utah consistently ranks among the highest in the nation for volunteerism. That spirit of giving back bolsters entrepreneurship. Dozens of incubators exist with specific niches and missions, from university-based programs like the U's Lassonde Center and BYU's Rollins Center, to Sustainable Startups and the Salt Mine. Some of these entities were founded by entrepreneurs as a way to give back, including Utah Jazz owners Gail and Larry Miller's entrepreneurship campus at Salt Lake Community College, BoomStartUp, Beehive StartUp, LaunchUp and the Women's Tech Council. Impact investing has a strong foothold in Utah, too. Sorenson Impact, where I work, has facilitated $100 million in investments in social enterprises across the globe."

Which is why Rise of the Rest chose to host the opening breakfast on our 2016 Salt Lake City tour at an unusual location—the Utah State Prison.

Breakfast is usually the time of day when we'll convene anywhere from twenty-five to one hundred leaders from a cross section of the community. We want to create the local experience where you have elected officials, heads of universities, CEOs of major corporations, together with leaders from the startup community. We bring together the early-stage founders who will be pitching later in the day for the $100,000 investment.

So, bright and early we gathered at the prison, which was

scheduled to be relocated and the site converted to a new tech hub. We were joined by a high-profile group that included then-mayor Ben McAdams (now a member of Congress), county officials, state leadership, tech company leaders (including representatives from eBay, Google, Adobe, and Ancestry.com), successful entrepreneurs, and LDS leaders. We hosted the breakfast at a small café on-site, called the Serving Time Café, where we were served by female inmates. The mission of the Serving Time Café is to help inmates plan and prepare for their future and the kind of work they might do—including building their own businesses.

When we'd been thinking about how to get these high-level guests fired up about innovation and entrepreneurship—and maybe make them a little bit uncomfortable too—we chose Serving Time as our venue, and were rewarded by some of the most thoughtful conversations we've had about building entrepreneurial communities for *all* the people. Over scrambled eggs and sausage links served on paper plates, we held an inspiring kickoff conversation. It was quickly apparent that many of the servers were themselves entrepreneurs—they'd just never had a chance to show it. They were paying the price for breaking the law, but looking to rebuild their lives when they were released and grab the chance they'd not been given before. It was a reminder that our mission of leveling the playing field and creating opportunities for people in more places—including those with diverse and often challenging backgrounds—remained vital.

We were motivated as we left the breakfast to create new on-ramps for entrepreneurship, and eager to hit the road and experience the city and meet some of the innovative companies as well as others on the front lines.

The experience is always unique to the locale, and it's often moving. For example, in Salt Lake City we went to a food warehouse called Rico Brands, founded by Jorge Fierro, a Mexican American immigrant. When he came to Salt Lake City, Jorge was homeless for a time and he didn't speak English, but he knew one thing—the Mexican food available wasn't up to his standards. He decided to do something about it and got his start selling beans at the Salt Lake Farmers Market. From there he grew it into a multimillion-dollar business, which has generated tremendous economic opportunity. Jorge is a natural collaborator who has created his own food ecosystem, helping new food ventures by preparing their products in his kitchen. During our visit we used his warehouse as a backdrop for a larger conversation.

We brought in an organization called Spice Kitchen Incubator, which was working with immigrants and refugees to help them adapt to American society, culture, and life in Salt Lake City through entrepreneurship in the food space. We had a gathering that included a group of early-stage entrepreneurs, and we went around and asked them to introduce themselves and talk about their businesses. It was very emotional and meaningful, and one of them in particular, Chef Donovan, the Jamaican-born owner of Jamaica's Kitchen, brought everyone to tears with his heartfelt expression of gratitude for being in America and having such remarkable business support, including meeting the Rise of the Rest team. He had always dreamed of having his own restaurant, and he found Salt Lake to be the most supportive community. A year after our visit, Chef Donovan launched Salt Lake's first Jamaican food truck, which has become wildly popular. Perhaps he's on the way toward birthing the next great restaurant concept. After all, Starbucks started as a single coffee shop in Seattle, Chipotle as a single burrito bar in Denver, and Sweetgreen as a single salad restaurant in Washington, DC. Sometimes businesses that seem small can be big, if the entrepreneurs get the right mentorship, and are able to raise capital to expand.

The "Doing Good" Startup Founder

Davis Smith will tell you that he wasn't one of those kids starting little homegrown businesses and dreaming of becoming an entrepreneur. In fact, it never occurred to him to be an entrepreneur. What he did want to do was make an impact. His father, who had once served as a missionary, moved the family to Latin America when Davis was a child. "I grew up knowing that I wanted to find a way to use my life to do good, to make the world a better place." After high school, Davis spent two years as a missionary in Bolivia, one of the poorest countries in the western hemisphere, and his commitment deepened. "I lived in little communities where I saw heartbreaking, devastating poverty that I think most Americans don't even understand exists, and when I got back, as a twenty-one-year-old going to college, I knew my purpose. I knew why I existed."

Davis wasn't sure what he would do with his sense of purpose. But while at college at Brigham Young University, he met an entrepreneur who had started a philanthropic organization, fighting poverty. Davis wanted to work for his nonprofit, but the philanthropist convinced him he should become an entrepreneur himself. After graduating from Wharton, he joined his cousin, a Harvard grad, in building an e-commerce business in Brazil.

One spring night in 2013, he was lying in bed in Brazil

thinking about his goals and feeling unsettled. He'd made a New Year's resolution that in 2013 he wanted to change somebody's life, and he hadn't done that. "I was feeling discouraged," he said. "My whole life had been focused on doing good and I hadn't figured out how to do it yet." He got out of bed and spent the entire night, the next day, and a second night thinking and planning. And from that he came up with the idea of a business that could sustainably do good while using profits to alleviate poverty. Davis's love of the outdoors was a key to the opportunity he began to imagine. "I felt there was space to build a brand in the outdoor industry and felt people who connected with the outdoors had connected with something bigger than themselves and would relate to this mission of doing good."

That was the basis for Cotopaxi, a startup named after a volcanic mountain in Ecuador where he'd lived as a teenager, which would sell "gear for good." The giving/impact aspect went beyond the more typical buy-one-give-one model. A percentage of Cotopaxi revenues is directed to a foundation Davis set up for the purpose of ending poverty.

Cotopaxi also seeks to make a positive impact every step of the way, exploring what it means to act ethically during each phase of a product's life. That means ensuring human rights throughout the supply chain, sourcing alternative materials, and committing to create all products using repurposed, recycled, and responsible materials by 2025.

When Davis was thinking about building the brand, he considered Silicon Valley and Seattle—both tech centers that had active outdoor cultures. But, ultimately, he decided that Salt Lake City was the best fit—the cost of living was lower, it was a dedicated outdoors community, and the underlying theme of doing good was very strong. He would soon discover that the tech startup community had knit together a strong support network that rallied around the efforts of entrepreneurs. That was especially important when Davis started piling up rejections from venture capitalists. They all loved the idea, but the giving aspect gave people pause. "I think it was because we were committed to giving away money before our company was profitable," he said.

Cotopaxi was one of our stops on the Salt Lake City tour, and we later invested in the company, which has continued to grow, raising $45 million in Series C funding in 2021. The company creed is "Do Good," and they've demonstrated that you really can do well while doing good.

NASHVILLE: Making Entrepreneurial Music

There's a reason I keep coming back to Nashville. When Rise of the Rest first stopped there as part of our very first tour in 2014, it was a geographical departure from the three other cities we'd chosen for that tour—Detroit, Cincinnati, and Pittsburgh. But I was eager to discover why it was ringing so many bells when it came to entrepreneurial innovation.

Nashville might not be the first place that comes to mind when people think of tech hubs, but actually it has a rich history of entrepreneurship, along with one of the most energetic startup communities anywhere in the country. It's a large city, with 1.6 million people, and fast-growing industries. Surprisingly, the largest industry is not music but health care, contributing $30 billion per year and 200,000 jobs to the local economy. This signals Nashville's promise as a startup hub. Before visiting we'd already had a glimpse of it.

Rise of the Rest managing partner David Hall put his finger on why Nashville is such a welcoming environment for startups, especially in the music and health care sectors: "What Nashville does really well is help these businesses coalesce around some of the natural industries in Nashville," he said. "So, health care and entertainment make so much sense, and there's such a great network of people that can be supportive to young startups that need been-there-done-that expertise around the table." Exactly. When you have a supportive community, it's invaluable.

We pulled into town late at night on June 26, 2014, and rose early in time for an 8:00 a.m. date at the Polk Center for the Nashville Technology Council Annual Meeting. The Nashville skyline glowed in the sunlight, a blend of old and new that felt crafted by artists. I thought of how many people had driven there following their dreams and had fallen in love with this beautiful city.

At the Polk Center I assured the crowd of five hundred people that, contrary to popular belief, I wasn't engaged in a battle with Silicon Valley. "I love Silicon Valley," I told them. "It is awesome and will continue to be awesome." It wasn't a zero-sum game. The point, I explained to them, was not to put down Silicon Valley but to lift up other areas of the country like Nashville that are doing amazing things and deserve attention and investment.

I was constantly impressed by Nashville's commitment to supporting entrepreneurs. With Rise of the Rest in town, it was all-hands-on-deck, from the governor on down. Governor Bill Haslam (in office between 2011 and 2019) was a true partner for entrepreneurs in Tennessee. He believed in them and backed that up with support. His family had great success in business, having founded the Pilot Flying J truck stop chain, so he knew the power of business and entrepreneurship.

Michael Burcham was also instrumental. Michael is an entrepreneur and investor with a long list of successes. I'd first met him when I was leading Startup America—he'd headed up the Startup Tennessee effort.

When Startup America was announced in early 2011, Michael wasted no time in contacting us. He helped make Tennessee the second region, after Illinois, to join Startup America. The excitement generated by the White House launch of Startup America allowed Michael to request that the governor support the rollout of the Nashville entrepreneurship center model across the state. The goal was that no one in the state should be more than one hour's drive from an entrepreneurship center.

Now Michael was CEO of the Nashville Entrepreneur Center, which he'd turned into a major startup incubator. In a five-year period, the launch of 114 startups had been supported by the center, and that helped put Nashville on the startup map, as one of the top entrepreneur hubs in the country.

The day was a whirlwind, with an unprecedented number of startup visits. We began our tour at Marathon Village, where we could feel the history. Parts of Marathon Village were built as early as 1881, and the Marathon automobile was produced there from 1910 to 1914. When that went out of business, the Marathon Village site languished for decades until a restoration began in 1986. The 130,000-square-foot factory houses Antique Archaeology, local radio station WRLT-FM Lightning 100, the Corsair Distillery, and more than fifty startups.

The Trolley Barns at Rolling Mill Hill was another hub, a burgeoning live-work community located in downtown Nashville's SoBro District (short for "south of Broadway"), a locus of ingenuity, energy, creativity, and technology. Rolling Mill Hill's creative campus, anchored by six early-twentieth-century trolley barns, houses a collective of Nashville's most creative and intelligent minds and fosters exchange between these artists, entrepreneurs, philanthropists, technologists, and business leaders.

The BowTruss Building, named for the curved steel trusses that support the vaulted roof, located in historic Germantown, has become a creative hub. And, of course, the Nashville Entrepreneur Center, Michael's signature hub of innovation.

One thing is clear. To be in Music City is to be transported back in time to the height of the Grand Ole Opry, which was founded at the iconic Ryman Auditorium in 1892. It's to soak up a century of country music—142 stars inducted into the Country Music Hall of Fame, from Hank Williams to Jimmy Dean, to Tammy Wynette, to Reba McEntire, to Kenny Rogers, to Clint Black, to Garth Brooks. Country music is a particular brand of Americana, but Nashville represents the fluidity of taste. Many classic rockers have gravitated to the city and made it their home as well, including Peter Frampton, Jack White, Sheryl Crow, John Oates, and Steven Tyler.

In the past, neighborhood revival and cultural change were often driven by the presence of a strong artistic community. Art and music brought a spirit of creative openness that ultimately translated into fresh economic energy. Today's variation on that theme is tech startups, and Nashville is now far more than a "music city" because of them.

A Musical Founder's Story

A decade ago, Mike Butera was a sometime-sociology professor and band member living on Music Row, a place where music companies and studios tend to congregate in the heart of Nashville. Mike, who had earned a master's degree in philosophy and a PhD in sound studies at Virginia Tech, had always been attracted by the way people embraced music. He dreamed of being able to play every part of a song, and he often carried around multiple instruments. The idea that nagged at him was: What if technology could be used to make the experience of playing music available to all?

Serious and soft-spoken, with a quiet but steady intensity, Mike spent years developing his invention, which he called Instrument 1—a piece of equipment designed to connect to one of hundreds of apps, creating a multi-instrument that anyone could play. As Mike described it, it could be whatever you wanted it to be—a guitar, a violin, a piano—you could basically be the entire band.

Mike's invention and his company, Artiphon, appealed to my interest in opening up opportunities for all. Here was a guy who was introducing the joy of making music to everybody. His goal was simple but profound: "I want to make beginners feel like pros and pros feel like beginners, for artists to have a new sense of wonder and beginners to immediately feel like they're making great music." The sociology professor in him recognized that when people are able to make music, they can access their emotions and express themselves more fully. He lit up when he described the potential of teaching music to kids using Instrument 1.

I was also impressed by Mike's early achievement, raising $1.3 million in Kickstarter crowdfunding money from people in seventy countries. That's especially impressive when you consider how difficult it can be to introduce new hardware. Artiphon is literally the invention of a new musical instrument.

A STATE OF REINVENTION

I returned to Nashville on my book tour in 2016, and participated in an interesting conversation with John Ingram, the chairman of Ingram Content Group, the Nashville-based global book supplier that was being challenged to stretch its boundaries and reinvent itself. The previous year Ingram had launched an accelerator program called 1440, named for the year Johannes Gutenberg invented the printing press. "Two thirds of the time it's been the most interesting of times," John told me. "The other third of the time it's probably been the most terrifying of times."

In the years after these visits, Nashville continued to distinguish itself—as did the entire state. In 2018, Powderkeg, an Indianapolis-based startup support organization with national reach, released its Tech Census report on Tennessee, surveying more than two hundred tech founders, employees, investors, and other tech leaders in Tennessee. The report's findings: 65 percent of startups surveyed had raised capital, 14 percent had accessed state or local growth incentives, and 37 percent of respondents were most bullish on the potential for health tech to boom over the next five years. In 2018, Tennessee startups raised $819 million, led by Nashville-based SmileDirectClub's $380 million fundraise.

Inspired by the startup culture of Tennessee, Rise of the Rest returned to the state in 2018 to tour Memphis, which has notable music chops of its own—known as the Birthplace of Rock and Roll and the Home of the Blues. We had a chance to experience that culture with a visit to the legendary Soul label Stax Records, which is co-located with a charter school focused on music education. It was inspiring to watch a class of mostly

Black musicians creating a new legacy at the site of a fifty-year-old record company. As it turned out, the winner of our pitch competition was a music company with a Black founder. Soundways, now Sound Credit, was founded by Gebre Waddell in 2016 as an audio technology platform that addresses every stage of music development and licensing. It positions itself as a music industry disrupter, bringing more transparency to the contributions of artists and technicians.

The juxtaposition of old and new was on display throughout our tour. Joining us was Fred Smith, the renowned founder, chairman, and CEO of Fedex, who built his company in Memphis. Fedex was a breakaway star of the 1970s and '80s that disrupted the U.S. Postal Service. It was meaningful to see Memphis's major business disrupter of forty years ago mingling with and advising the young, new disrupters of today.

TAMPA BAY REGION: Reviving a Downtown

In 2010, when investor Jeff Vinik, former head of the Fidelity Magellan mutual fund, was considering purchasing the Tampa Bay Lightning, the hockey team was on the verge of bankruptcy. Looking around, Jeff could see that its hometown was on the ropes as well. Yet there was something about Tampa that appealed to him as a place he could see himself living. He had the vision to understand its potential and the commitment to put his money and his energy behind the task. Not only did he buy the team but he made a big bet on the city—a $3 billion live-work-play development that is transforming Tampa's downtown area.

Jeff is an example of a new trend we've seen with investors.

That is, they don't just back startups, they invest in the surrounding real estate to build a community that helps entrepreneurs thrive. This strategy helps communities win the battle
for talent, as people are drawn by the amenities, the lifestyle,
and the support system. As one of the top investors of the last
half century, Jeff is a true innovator who can see the big picture.

Jeff's concept, called Water Street Tampa, was designed to
include residences, hotels, a medical school, an entertainment
complex, retail space, and, hopefully, a major corporate headquarters. It's an example of what live-work-play is all about.

Most interesting about the development is its cutting-edge
attention to health and well-being. It will be the first WELL certified community in the world, one that functions to promote
health and well-being across all aspects of community life by
being inclusive, integrated, and resilient, and by fostering high
levels of social engagement. This unique lifestyle will be available to those working, living, or entertaining in Water Street
Tampa.

The entrepreneurial core of the project is the Embarc Collective, an innovation hub dedicated to supporting startups. The
Embarc Collective is fully staffed with advisers and experts to
deliver a high-level standard of support to entrepreneurs. All of
this will take place in a spacious state-of-the-art facility, which
will meet the needs and help fulfill the dreams of Tampa's
startup community.

When Rise of the Rest visited the Tampa Bay/St. Petersburg
region in 2019 we were enveloped in a spirit of excitement and
promise. Jeff praised the area's vitality and its growth, promising that "ten years from now, there will be another 25 percent

more people here than there are now. That's 25 percent more demand for the theater, for hockey tickets, for a company's services, for condos. It's an incredible tailwind to have."

In our fireside chat Jeff found a colorful way to build an entrepreneurial analogy with ice hockey, pointing out that building a startup requires a strong guard who can protect the rest of your players. "It all comes down to people. . . . And there is nothing harder than being a founder, than being a startup, than working on a shoestring budget. You're going to have the door slammed in your face. If you're not resilient . . . it's the same with hockey players. They go through ups and downs, and struggle with disappointment. But they pick themselves up and come back with renewed effort and passion to win."

I agreed with Jeff's analogy. "With sports, the difference between success and failure can sometimes be a millisecond. Sometimes it's one wrong move, or perhaps just bad luck. It's not that different with startups," I told the gathering. "It's getting that break with a customer, or an investor. I lived this firsthand, with AOL. We almost didn't make it. We struggled, we went through layoffs. It got to the point where I got a call from my parents, urging me to put my startup dreams aside and take a safer corporate job. But after some bad breaks we got some good breaks. And we went from almost dying to suddenly succeeding. If you're an entrepreneur, you can't give up. And if there's a barrier in front of you, you just have to go around it, or over it, or knock it down."

"Are you committed?" Jeff asked the audience. "Do you have the personality to be a founder where you may not know what your day will bring next and where you're going to go—but you keep going?"

By the way, the Lightning won the Stanley Cup in both 2020 and 2021. No question, Jeff Vinik is on to something. Tampa is on the rise, and so is St. Pete, now the home of investment firms ARK and Dynasty, both of which relocated their headquarters from New York City to St. Pete in recent years.

PART TWO

ENTREPRENEURS DRIVING THE FUTURE

NINE

The Waves Converge

In *The Third Wave*, I wrote about the first two waves of the internet—the first, creating the ability to connect online; and the second, building software, such as search and social networking, on top of the internet. The Third Wave is where the internet meets the real world, and starts impacting our everyday lives, our businesses, and our communities in even more profound ways.

Although it's only been a few years, it feels like a lifetime ago since I first wrote about the Third Wave. Many of the predictions I made are coming true. Yet I don't think I or anyone else fully appreciated the scope of the transformation that would occur with "the internet of everything," most of all during the pandemic, when overnight the entire world pivoted to fully embrace the internet in almost every aspect of their lives.

In the years after I wrote *The Third Wave*, people would ask me, "What's the next wave?" I'd duck the question, as I really didn't have a good response, and I thought the Third Wave dynamics would take two decades to fully play out, just as the internet's first and second waves had.

But the pandemic and the speed at which it drove transformation finally gave me the glimmers of an answer. It is clear that a very powerful dynamic has kicked in, building on some trends that had been bubbling for years, but things really took flight during the pandemic, which has led to a fundamental reassessment of virtually every aspect of business, and life.

It is increasingly clear that four trends are now gaining strength, and as they build and converge, they likely will reshape our lives in ways we might not yet fully understand. Each of the four is giving expression to a movement, and while every one of them is powerful in its own right, the key is not so much the individual impact of any of them but rather the larger and multiplying impact of the convergence of *all* of them.

This convergence not only serves to accelerate the individual trends. It creates a once-in-a-generation *megatrend*—a likely tidal wave that has the potential to dramatically reshape our world, in immeasurable ways.

So perhaps *that's* the fourth wave—a converging tidal wave that goes well beyond merely the next phase of the internet, that instead upends many aspects of our lives, reshapes the economy, and may—just may—also help unify our divided country.

The four big trends that are each now building strength, and starting to converge, are:

1. The emergence of tech centers around industry expertise.
2. The rise of more job-creating startup hubs.
3. The pandemic-fueled acceleration of innovation trends.
4. The increased engagement of government as a catalyst.

Let's examine each of them.

I. The Emergence of Tech Centers around Industry Expertise

As a perpetual outlier whose internet startup AOL was not based in Silicon Valley but in the Washington, DC, region—the seat of government and often the antithesis of disruption—I'm well versed in the view that Silicon Valley has always been the epicenter of America's technology engine. However, it would probably surprise people to learn that Silicon Valley's dominance is fairly recent. During the first wave of the internet there was a broad geographical distribution: AOL in DC, Dell in Austin, Sprint in Kansas City, IBM in Boca Raton, CompuServe in Columbus, Hayes Modems in Atlanta.

So, we've seen this movie before. A wide range of cities helped get America online in the internet's First Wave but became less relevant in the Second Wave. In the Third Wave, many are roaring back.

It isn't that tech mavens will swoop in from the coasts to save the day. The magic of innovation across the nation will emerge when people from different places come together to share their critical expertise. During that Second Wave of the internet, when the focus was on software, it made some sense that technical leaders like Mark Zuckerberg and Jack Dorsey would congregate in Silicon Valley. There was no particular regional angle, or local or industry expertise needed.

In the Third Wave, tech opportunities in fields ranging from health care to farming, from transportation to housing, will require more subject-matter expertise, much of which exists in cities all across America. New ideas will flourish as a result of the relationships among tech employees, executives, and investors who become woven into noncoastal locales. And the strength of those bonds will attract investors and partners to many of these budding ventures.

Mark Muro, metropolitan policy director at the Brookings Institution, was an early voice in spreading support for tech innovation across the country. His research noted that since the 1980s there has been a trend toward "divergence"—separating top-tier tech hubs on the coasts from the rest of the nation. "The result is a crisis of regional imbalance," Muro concluded in a paper he wrote in 2019 with Robert D. Atkinson and Jacob Whiton titled "The Case for Growth Centers: How to Spread Tech Innovation Across America." The authors observed, "Among the superstar metro areas, the winner-take-most dynamics of the innovation economy have led to dominance but also livability and competitiveness crises: spiraling real estate costs, traffic gridlock, and increasingly uncompetitive wage and salary costs. Meanwhile, in many of the 'left-behind places,' the struggle to keep up has brought stagnation and frustration. These uneven realities represent a serious productivity, competitiveness, and equity problem."

Like me, Mark woke up to the fact that innovation isn't happening everywhere, and he asked what could be done about it. He started by learning from the past.

"Regions didn't always matter as much," Mark told us for the book. "Before 1980, economic success had more to do with whether you had a river or an ocean port, or a repository of iron work. But otherwise, most places were pretty much the same, and were becoming more of the same. That's what we call economic convergence.

"Technology changed things, as it put an emphasis on concentrations of highly skilled people. There was a lot of distress in the places that were left behind, epitomized by the drug crisis. You can't run an economy where most people feel that the action is somewhere else."

This dissatisfaction and division were reflected in politics as well, including in the election of Donald Trump, who billed his presidential run as a way to give voice to people who felt disrespected and left behind. But Mark had been looking at these issues for a long time, and he knew that this dynamic was not just about politics. "We all agree on the importance of innovation, but it won't work if people think it's only occurring in San Francisco and New York, or Boston," he said. "And what this is about, fundamentally, is a more healthy and inclusive understanding. And if we don't do that, we're going to lose our edge. If most people think that the cool stuff is happening somewhere else, they're ultimately not going to support it. They'll turn on it, and we'll lose our ability as a nation to compete with rising powers like China."

In fairness it must be said that San Francisco, New York, and Boston earned their status on the leading edge of tech innovation. San Francisco became a place of single-minded dedication to invention and experimentation. Along the way it developed an understanding of how to allocate and price risk, so people have permission to take risks to push the boundaries of what's possible. New York City is a global magnet—the center of finance, media, and the arts, and a cutting-edge tech hub. Boston, with its storied academic and research capabilities, is the place to go to solve the hard problems, particularly around biotech. These cities established leadership early, and their momentum enables them to continue to be magnets for top talent, much as a celebrated college sports team is often best able to attract the most promising high school athletes. The leads that San Francisco, New York City, and Boston have are strong and durable, and they will no doubt continue to launch some of the most innovative companies. The rise of the rest does not imply the fall of the leaders, but rather more cities rising up in relevance and importance. And the point isn't necessarily to catch up or overcome the prominence of San Francisco, New York City, and Boston. It's for places like Detroit or Miami to flex their regional advantages and carve out their own exceptionalism. And there are many paths available for them to do it.

The recent rise of some of America's emerging tech cities was sometimes unexpected. Seattle would never have become a tech hub had not Bill Gates and Paul Allen happened to grow up there. When they initially started Microsoft, they were in Albuquerque, but they decided to move home to Seattle. What began as a ten-person company is now a major tech hub. And the only reason Amazon started in Seattle is because Microsoft was there. Jeff Bezos famously drove across the country and set up shop in Seattle because he wanted to hire Microsoft engineers to build Amazon.

Dell launched in Austin because that's where Michael Dell was living at the time. He went to school there and started the company out of his dorm room and then kept growing. Dell helped Austin gain a reputation as an innovative city, which in turn gave rise to an infusion of culture that inspired South by Southwest (SXSW), the massive festival and conference. SXSW features film, music, culture, and tech, and its role in highlighting new tech trends and promoting and connecting startups with venture capital can't be overstated. More than any other festival or conference, SXSW has established itself as the standard, and the place to see and be seen—in the process, making Austin more of a startup city.

Increasingly we're finding startup hubs emerging around existing regional and industry strengths. In these cases, they're often advantaged because they're *not* in Silicon Valley. We've seen this in the new startup hubs developing around health care, agriculture, and transportation. For example, there has been a surge in startups in areas near medical hubs, such as Minnesota with the Mayo Clinic, and Baltimore with Johns Hopkins University.

2. The Rise of More Job-Creating Startup Hubs

As we've found, startups tend to be more successful when they operate within innovation ecosystems—with Silicon Valley being the most iconic.

The ecosystem model is a striking change from the historic concept of pioneers as lone wolves. The most successful emerging ecosystems recognize that scaling a startup requires network density—being in close, regular contact with other creators who share a willingness to explore what is possible and help each other succeed.

According to Andy Stoll, who leads Ecosystem Development at the Kauffman Foundation, "Entrepreneurship and innovation have been democratized. That means if you have an idea you want to create, the barriers to entry have started to collapse. And networks are replacing hierarchies." That means more people have a chance to move from idea to execution in creating businesses.

In *The Third Wave* I asked readers to imagine a time when a city like New Orleans might emerge as a startup hub. At the time, many readers likely thought that was unrealistic, maybe even fanciful. But that's what is happening, not just in New

Orleans (which recently birthed a unicorn analytics company called Lucid that we backed) but in dozens of cities throughout the country. And the pandemic has become a tipping point for this movement, accelerating the dispersion of talent and capital. This will unleash a wave of innovation, as the entrepreneurs in these rising cities build on their experiences to improve many of the most important aspects of our lives.

Richard Florida, a leading analyst, author, and educator who has been studying the future of cities for decades, wrote for Bloomberg in March 2022 that while a small group of cities still dominate as tech hubs, more cities are starting to benefit from a heightened investment in innovation. He wrote, "One thing is clear from the data so far: The real silver lining is that the huge national surge in venture capital and tech jobs means that many places are seeing real growth of their startup ecosystems and broader high-tech industries. When it comes to the geography of American innovation, a proverbial rising tide may at long last be lifting more boats."

The benefits of innovators clustering together have been clear for centuries. More than 1,500 years ago, Venice became the leader in glassmaking. In his book *How We Got to Now: Six Innovations That Made the Modern World*, Steven Johnson noted that "by concentrating glassmakers on a single island, Venice triggered a surge in creativity." So, the idea of Silicon Valley, or network density, is certainly not new. What's new is the idea that dozens of cities can build innovation clusters, not just a few.

3. The Pandemic-Fueled Acceleration of Innovation Trends

Our fear at the start of the pandemic was that it would undo some of the momentum building around early-stage startups and rising cities. Instead, the opposite happened. Times of crisis often lead to periods of great innovation, and this is true now. Notably, there have been signs of a shift in the flow of talent to cities and towns across the country. Where once tech innovators felt obligated to be on the coasts, the pandemic has accelerated the boomerang of people returning home.

The COVID pandemic has led many to conclude that physical density may not matter in the future. Zoom and other technologies have enabled people to work together even if they are physically distributed. A growing number of startups have adopted a "fully remote" strategy, hiring people from all across the world, without having a central office they go to. The success of open-source technologies and collaborative tools has made this more possible, and no doubt there will be more of these highly distributed companies in the future.

But place will continue to matter, and clustering people together so they can feed off each other, not just in planned ways but in serendipitous ways, will still be the way it works for most companies, and most cities. The greater awareness about the ability to work remotely will likely drive more people to choose to live in different cities, but once in those cities, they no doubt will look to make connections with others in the community.

One trend is unmistakable: In 2021, the "Great Resignation" led to an average of 3.9 million people leaving their jobs every month. In a related statistic, one in four workers said they're planning to look for a new job when the pandemic ends. Some of that will come from people who decided to stay in—or return to—their hometowns.

Increasingly, these returnees are discovering that they can pursue their tech innovations right where they are, and most of them will find other entrepreneurs nearby doing similar things.

This experience has confirmed what we've discovered on our bus tours across America. (Reddit cofounder Alexis Ohanian noticed that too, and in the middle of the pandemic he tweeted that Rise of the Rest "is really looking prophetic now.")

Where you live and where you work have historically largely been a bundled offering. We might now be at the moment where work and life are functionally being unbundled, creating unparalleled flexibility. Along with that, startups within the Rise of the Rest cities (those outside the Bay Area, New York, and Boston) are experiencing an acceleration of opportunity. At Revolution we polled our Rise of the Rest Seed Fund portfolio, and we learned that pre-COVID only 20 percent of the companies we had backed had remote work options. Now more than 70 percent plan to institute some remote options or shift to fully remote environments.

Many people are now talking about the COVID-19 pandemic as a revolution, exposing societal weaknesses and leading to great, and potentially irreversible, changes in how and where we live, work, learn, and play.

In some cases, that's true. But with many other things, it's more of an accelerator—albeit a big one—of the existing tech/innovation/demographic trends that have been at work for decades, and which we've experienced firsthand through Rise of the Rest.

The pandemic has also given rise to advances in health and education, as well as many lifestyle changes. It looks as if some of the solutions put in place for the pandemic are here to stay. Technologies that had been available for decades, but had seen slow adoption, suddenly were adopted by every business and every classroom. There was also a dramatic, overnight shift in terms of how health care is delivered, particularly the adoption of telehealth, which has given consumers better access to their doctors through virtual office visits. That was essential when doctor's offices were largely closed, but doctors and patients have realized that there are long-term benefits to this option, which can potentially improve the quality of care by making it more accessible. New technologies also help patients become active participants in their health care, initially around in-home testing related to COVID, but with broader and more sustainable innovations quickly building momentum. Talkspace, a telehealth company delivering online therapy that we backed, saw a dramatic rise in interest during the pandemic.

E-commerce has accelerated quite significantly, and that's likely to continue as people grow accustomed to the convenience and infinite variety. The same is true of restaurant delivery and takeout options, which will remain popular because it's something people enjoy as a convenient alternative to a seated restaurant. Movie theaters were already struggling before the pandemic, and the ubiquity of streaming services makes that a trend that will likely continue. People will still go to restaurants and movie theaters, for the immersive social experience they provide, but the easy, less expensive, at-home options will take permanent root.

As schools went to remote learning, many new companies emerged focused on K–12. Again, this was an explosive acceleration of a more gradual trend. Back in 2015 when Rise of the Rest conducted a national pitch competition at SXSW, the winner was the Iowa City startup Pear Deck, an interactive education tool. Pear Deck was growing steadily, but it really exploded during the pandemic.

So has DC-based Class Technologies, started in the early months of the pandemic by serial entrepreneur Michael Chasen.

Michael's frustrations with the difficulties his kids were having with online at-home learning led him to launch Class to customize Zoom for classrooms. Less than a year after starting the company, the momentum Michael had in the market led Soft-Bank to invest $75 million in Class, turning it into a billion-dollar valuation unicorn.

As I mentioned earlier, I'm the chair of the Smithsonian Institution. The museums closed to physical traffic during much of the pandemic, but in a greater sense the museums never closed. We heightened our digital efforts and created a virtual Smithsonian, which is always open. What a wonderful opportunity to take the Smithsonian to every classroom and every household. Now all Americans can experience some of its wonders without ever leaving home.

The pandemic has also energized the entrepreneurial community nationwide. The U.S. Census Bureau reported that in 2021, 5.4 million new business applications were filed. Some studies suggest that Gen Z (people born between 1997 and 2012) is driving the trend. One survey by EY Ripples and JA Worldwide found that 53 percent of Gen Z respondents aspired to run their own businesses one day, with the number spiking to 65 percent for those who were already in the workforce. Digitally skilled Gen Z entrepreneurs are emerging as important players in startup ecosystems in every region of the country.

4. The Increased Engagement of Government as a Catalyst

For most of the last two centuries the United States was at the forefront of every great drive for innovation. We led the way with the Agricultural Revolution. We led the way again with the

Industrial Revolution. More recently, we led the way with the Digital Revolution.

A big reason is that as a nation we committed fully to investing in the future. For example, in 1960, the United States was responsible for almost 70 percent of the R&D spending globally. You can draw a direct line from this investment to the technological advances that came from the space program and the invention of the internet.

Today, that picture is much different. Our investment has sunk to only 30 percent of global R&D. Other countries are figuring out that embracing the future and investing in R&D is a good strategy. As the United States has drawn down, they've stepped up.

It's too bad there isn't a greater sense of urgency. Government initiatives are crucial, and they also provide an opportunity to expand the innovation economy to lift every region of the country. But what happens *within* each community is even *more* important.

There can sometimes be a tension between the innovation community and government. From the innovators' standpoint, government is sluggish, risk-averse, and even broken. Look at the never-ending debate over high-skilled immigration. Leaders on both sides of the aisle have called for stapling green cards to PhDs for more than a decade, so students who come to the United States for graduate studies can stay, but the politics of immigration has led to a stalemate, and many of these bright innovators are forced to leave. More recently, there has been a lot of focus on increasing America's competitiveness. In 2021 the Senate passed the US Innovation and Competition Act, and the House passed a similar America COMPETES bill, but there's been an impasse in getting an integrated bill passed.

(During his 2022 State of the Union address, President Biden renamed them the Bipartisan Innovation Act, so hopefully that will create more momentum toward passage.) People in government argue that they're trying to do the right thing, but unlike businesses, which can be far more nimble, they are subject to accountability to a large and diverse population, with various needs. Not to mention the political considerations, which can stymie the most sound efforts.

It took a while for startups to get serious attention from policymakers, largely because public interest was higher for small businesses. The government had spent decades hammering home the message that small businesses were the core of American commerce and the key to the future. Even when government initiatives focused on high-growth startups, the language in the announcements was often about small businesses—because they had broader appeal and seemed less elitist.

But startups are a different animal. Startups start small, so initially they look like small businesses, but they aspire to be big, as they generally aim to grow rapidly and become significant engines of economic growth and job creation. But startups can't succeed on their own. They need a community that celebrates them, and they need to be able to access capital, and attract talent, to scale their ideas.

We've seen with Rise of the Rest that individual cities and states have made valiant efforts to create vibrant startup communities. But playing David in a world where Goliath—a few places like Silicon Valley—really dominates is a hard fight. While entrepreneurs need to lead, and investors need to back them, there's also a role for public policy to take steps to level the playing field. And these sorts of programs won't just help specific cities. They will maximize the likelihood that America can continue to lead as the world's preeminent innovation nation.

Some might think my views are a little naive, or Pollyanna-ish, but I truly believe that a key to unifying America has been—and will be—unleashing innovation and growth. That held true when it was an investment in railroads after the Civil War, or an investment in space in the divisive 1960s. It holds true today.

The new face of a potential private-public partnership is reflected in the work of Ro Khanna, the congressman who represents Silicon Valley. Born in Philadelphia in 1976 to parents who emigrated from India, he has written about his and his family's journey: "The cliché rings true for me: only in America is a story like mine possible."

One of Khanna's main platforms is the role of innovation and technology in America's future. In his 2022 book, *Dignity in a Digital Age: Making Tech Work for All of Us*, Khanna writes that "place matters. . . . We need place-based policymakers that extend twenty-first-century jobs beyond the current superstar cities to overlooked communities."

If anyone suspects that the congressman representing one of the wealthiest districts in America, which happens to be the tech capital, is merely paying lip service to the idea of tech equity across the nation, they should look at his record in Congress. Khanna is serious about using tech to create jobs and economic rebirth beyond Silicon Valley. Notably, in recent years Khanna, a Democrat, worked with Iowa's Republican governor, Kim Reynolds, to create a "digital forge" that would create coding jobs. Governor Reynolds has nothing but praise for Khanna, saying, "Ro Khanna has been a champion in our efforts to make

America's heartland a powerful force for the technological revolution." Khanna is promoting similar opportunities in other heartland states, noting:

> The United States has been the country of possibility for more than two centuries, leaning into the future, imagining a better world, and then rolling up its sleeves to make it happen. This effort requires constant vigilance. We need to double down on the weapon of progress that has enabled America to lead the world for the past two centuries. That weapon is our entrepreneurs—not just on the coasts, but all across the country.

Each of the four trends—the converging waves of cities with critical industry expertise, rising startup hubs, pandemic-related acceleration of technological and societal trends, and an all-of-government commitment to lead the future—is important. But what is most exciting to me is how they are now accelerating, and converging, in a way that provides unparalleled possibilities.

TEN

The Entrepreneurial Activists

In 2019, Rise of the Rest visited Puerto Rico, where the entrepreneurial community had been on the front lines during one of the more challenging comeback stories I've seen. In the aftermath of the severe hurricanes that devastated the island in recent years, Puerto Rico's startup support networks came together to help the island rebuild. Their prior experiences made the ecosystem uniquely positioned to respond quickly to the pandemic in a number of ways.

What made the response to catastrophe different was the determination of the entrepreneurial community to envision a more fundamental creation of building blocks for permanent development. For example, creating sustainable agriculture and energy production, which is a big deal as Puerto Rico imports more than 85 percent of its food, as well as addressing long-term infrastructure and transportation issues.

On the ground, entrepreneurs told us repeatedly that Hurricane Maria was a wakeup call, and entrepreneurs are building for a future of resiliency. We saw this with organizations such as Endeavor Puerto Rico and Parallel18, which are focused on providing entrepreneurs with the resources and tools needed to be successful on the island. We also visited Piloto 151, a leading coworking space that supports innovators.

After Hurricane Maria, José Andrés, the heroic entrepreneurial chef from Washington, DC, whose nonprofit, World Central Kitchen, has aided many communities during times of natural disaster, rushed to Puerto Rico where he served nearly four million meals to the devastated population. Afterward, José wanted to do something more sustainable, and that's how Plow to Plate came into being.

Plow to Plate is a World Central Kitchen grant program that supports and partners with agricultural organizations, small farms, and small businesses to create a sustainable food economy. When we visited food operations with José on our 2019 tour, we were encouraged by the energy and resolve of the entrepreneurial community, and by how important this work is.

I had first met José in DC many years earlier, and invested in his ThinkFoodGroup, his restaurant holding company. José has a wonderful immigrant story. Coming to America by boat, he found his way into the back of a kitchen, started his own restaurant, and then built a restaurant empire with more than twenty restaurants in major cities around the world. His success as a chef and as an entrepreneur is widely known, as is his passion for feeding people in need, initially through DC Central Kitchen, and then through World Central Kitchen, which has emerged as one of the most successful nonprofit launches in history.

Like many, I was impressed by the way he was using his talent and energy to address hunger and come to the aid of those in need. He preached that food could be an agent of change, and in José's hands that was true.

José stepped up again when the pandemic hit, going on a mission "to feed the world" at a time when access to food was closed off for many. He told his staff that COVID might be the reason World Central Kitchen was created. "Every time we think big, we deliver," he said, which could be a motto for all entrepreneurs.

José was an early fan of Rise of the Rest and was tenacious in convincing us to visit Puerto Rico. He made me promise we'd eventually come, and in exchange, he promised to lead our efforts and join us on our tour.

When we arrived in February 2019, the resilience of Puerto Rico's entrepreneurial community was quickly evident. According to Endeavor Insight, Puerto Rico's tech industry has experienced rapid growth in recent years. Endeavor Insight's report showed that the vast majority of tech founders grew up or went to high school on the island, and they started their companies in response to a specific market opportunity or from a desire to give back to the community. However, many companies struggled to scale, and they needed to create the means of supporting the budding tech community. An example would be Parallel18, which we visited on the tour. Parallel18 is an international startup accelerator based in Puerto Rico. It supports and invests in eighty global companies a year with the goal of having an economic and social impact on the island.

At the accelerator Piloto 151's Santurce location we gathered together local investors—around fifty of them representing many different investment groups and angels. We were told that the first two startups in the accelerator—Abartys Health and Brands of Puerto Rico—had raised over $1 million. Abartys

Health, which provided a centralized communication platform for more accessible health care, went on to win the pitch competition and $100,000.

There is also support for entrepreneurs from other organizations. Foundation for Puerto Rico, a nonprofit dedicated to social and economic development, hosted a Rise of the Rest roundtable. Throughout the day we were inspired by the energy and drive of the Puerto Rican startup community. Time and again the entrepreneurs, most of whom were young, told us that *they* would be the engines of progress for Puerto Rico. In their lives they had already overcome natural disasters and struggle, and their determination and sense of community strengthened them. The startup community was on the rise.

Months after we visited Puerto Rico, where our attention had been on rebuilding after natural disaster, the COVID pandemic hit. For me, one of the great inspirational stories of the pandemic has been the way the tech ecosystems pivoted to help their communities survive and then recover.

OHIO'S INNOVATION FUND SUPPORTS SMALL BUSINESSES

Ohio is home to a large and robust economy, with a relatively high concentration of Fortune 1000 companies. Major corporate players include Cardinal Health, Kroger, Marathon Petroleum, Procter & Gamble, Nationwide, Progressive, and Macy's. Many of these companies do a great job of engaging with local startups—we certainly found that with P&G in Cincinnati when Rise of the Rest visited in 2014. The startup community is also strong and has been rising rapidly in recent years. The state's expertise in health care, anchored by Cardinal Health, was also demonstrated by McKesson's acquisition of Columbus-based CoverMyMeds for $1.1 billion.

Ohio's diverse business community immediately felt the effects of the pandemic, with companies such as Macy's laying off nearly 4,000 corporate workers, and Columbus-based Nationwide laying off or furloughing 600 employees. L Brands, the parent company of Victoria's Secret and Bath & Body Works, announced a 15 percent workforce reduction, which impacted 850 people at the company's Columbus headquarters. Small businesses and startups were also hit hard. By April 2020, seventy companies across Cincinnati had laid off a combined 16,000 workers. A variety of events that convene the Ohio startup community were canceled or postponed, including Startup Week festivities.

JobsOhio stepped into the breach. Since its launch in 2011, JobsOhio, a nonprofit funded by the state's liquor revenues, had been a strong supporter of startups, fulfilling its mission to drive job creation and new capital investment in Ohio through business attraction, retention, and expansion efforts. In 2019, JobsOhio reported working on 306 projects that helped create 22,770 new jobs across the state.

Before the pandemic, JobsOhio had been working on a program that would provide matching funds to complement venture capital investment in the state's startups. This initiative was called the JobsOhio Innovation Fund and was poised to launch just as the pandemic hit. Now JobsOhio quickly pivoted to COVID support, and customized the Innovation Fund to meet a more urgent purpose—providing capital to early-stage companies that would need an infusion of cash to survive. Complementing the federal aid provided by the CARES Act, the $50 million pool matched equity investments from private investors to help secure many of the state's venture-backed startups.

It was very clear that the purpose of the Innovation Fund was not just to create an emergency fix but, even in the midst of crisis, to fulfill its long-term objective of boosting venture capital investments in the state and create a sustainable startup ecosystem.

Between March and August 2020, all $50 million was deployed to fund thirty-seven businesses, with $63 million in additional matched capital (more than one-to-one). The result was a rescue of startups, with an estimated 1,200 jobs saved.

MINNEAPOLIS: "Do the Most Good"

One of the most dramatic examples of a collaborative community has been Minneapolis, and its strong response in 2020 did not surprise us.

A little background. When we chose Minneapolis for our second Rise of the Rest tour back in 2014, it was because this thriving metropolis had so many things to recommend it—natural beauty, a strong artistic community, and a solid economic foundation with more Fortune 500 companies per capita than any other US metro area—among them UnitedHealth, Target, Best Buy, 3M, and General Mills. It also included an impressive budding startup culture, especially notable in the health tech arena.

Senator Amy Klobuchar joined us on the tour. From the start, the senator was fully onboard with our mission. She believes in the power of startups, especially in their ability to attract talented young people to her state. In the years after our Rise of the Rest tour in Minnesota she would become a reliable champion, and in 2020 she'd introduce the New Business Preservation Act to create a federal partnership with states and private investors to encourage startups.

This and other successes distinguished the Minneapolis startup ecosystem. As far as ecosystems go, it had many important elements from the ecosystem wheel:

Investments? Check: In 2019 Minnesota's startups raised $1.2 billion, including from some leading venture firms in addition to Revolution, such as Bessemer Venture Partners, as well as early-stage venture funds like Matchstick Ventures, Great North Labs, and Bread & Butter Ventures.

Accelerators? Check: There are nearly thirty startup accelerator programs, such as Techstars United Healthcare, Techstars Farm to Fork, OnRamp Insurance Accelerator, and MN Cup. There is also Forge North, a coalition of entrepreneurs, investors, corporate innovators, and other support organizations.

Corporate support? Check: Many of the large corporations in the state, such as UnitedHealth, Target, and Best Buy, have supported startups.

But 2020 tested Minneapolis's strength, resolve, and community support system with the joint crises of COVID and the murder of George Floyd. Its response was to mount a rallying effort.

Notably, the Coven, a coworking space and community with locations in Minneapolis and Saint Paul, quickly rose to the pandemic challenge by creating digital programming for its members. Fix-It-Fridays, a virtual event series, was instantly popular. The weekly video call for entrepreneurs and community activists and leaders attracted more than one thousand attendees, and was a reprieve from the isolation and a much-needed mood booster. It was also a virtual accelerator, providing advice and inspiration for startups as they moved forward.

Floyd's murder was a shock to the community, and it cata-lyzed a different kind of momentum. The Coven pivoted to use its coworking space, which had been closed for the pandemic, to collect food and other donated items for the locals affected by the protests. Generous local donors, many of them from businesses, rose to the occasion, and volunteers flocked to the center to join the effort to gather, sort, and deliver hundreds of thousands of dollars' worth of emergency goods across the city.

The way the Coven founders described it, this community support was all a part of its original promise: "We pride our-selves on creating spaces which provide physical and psycho-logical safety for our members. That mission only became more important during a pandemic. Then, when George Floyd was murdered, we were compelled to act and address the needs of our neighbors—we didn't feel there was any other option. The way we saw it, contributing our resources to the fight for ra-cial justice in America, in whatever way we could, was and is the right thing to do. Our team and members came together to support one another in the name of community."

A Small Startup Learns a Pandemic Lesson

Supply chain management is the name of the game in our cur-rent environment, so the delivery management system intro-duced by the startup Dispatch is a welcome entry. As founder Andrew Leone described it, he and his partners started out in a grassroots manner some five years ago. "Homeowners wanted things done same day. And so we started running product out directly, just with our own vehicles, whenever they needed it. Customers would say, 'Whoever can get product to me when I need it, where I need it, can have all my business.' So, we said, 'Sure, we'll do that.'"

However, from the start it was a tough sell to venture capitalists. Five years in, it's very different. "We get emails almost daily from investors wanting to talk."

It was a long process to get there. Their original concept, running trucks and doing delivery directly to job sites, wasn't scalable. At that point they hit on the big idea—to build software to coordinate the logistics. Initially, they thought they'd just use it as an internal tool, but they soon discovered that everyone else had the same problem. And that's when the concept started to fall into place. "Our customer base evangelized it," Andrew said. "I had competitors calling me, wanting to use this software. So, I decided to step down from my operating role in this other business and go and build Dispatch."

Through the pandemic and then the supply chain crisis, Dispatch held steady, supported its workers, and did what it could to lift up its community. "Now," said Andrew, "you're seeing a ton of investment in technology in the distribution space, because they all know if a similar crisis happens again, they're going to fail. They don't have the margin to miss it again. So, you're seeing a lot more investing in e-commerce, in supply chain." He wondered, though, what would be possible if there weren't so many constraints in the supply chain. That was a question worth pursuing.

TULSA: The Mission Is to Be Helpful

It might seem kind of unusual for a venture capital firm to define its mission as "to be helpful," but that's what Michael

Basch had in mind when he created Atento Capital in Tulsa. "Most people don't associate Tulsa with innovation," Michael noted, but he saw potential in the historic bones of the city and the special ingenuity of the people. Tulsa is the true heartland.

The hub of tech innovation is 36 Degrees North, Tulsa's basecamp for entrepreneurs and startups, with a wide range of resources, work spaces, and a diverse, engaged community of entrepreneurs. The effort received major support from large local philanthropic institutions, the George Kaiser Family Foundation, and the Lobeck Taylor Family Foundation.

A great deal of Tulsa's startup momentum is attributable to the tireless efforts of George Kaiser, who has funded a range of initiatives including Tulsa Remote to attract employees, and the Woody Guthrie Museum to attract visitors. He also funded the $465 million Gathering Place Park, one of the largest and most ambitious public parks ever created with private funds, which perhaps as much as anything ratcheted up Tulsa's national visibility when it opened in 2018.

Tulsa was on the rise when the pandemic hit. In fact, we'd scheduled it for an upcoming Rise of the Rest bus tour, which had to be postponed. Suddenly, Tulsa was forced to shift gears from developing a thriving ecosystem to utilizing its existing ecosystem to protect the community—as Michael would put it, "to be helpful."

Looking for a way to pitch in during the pandemic, McKenna Raley, an intern with Atento, came up with the idea for TulsaResponds, an online platform that would enable Tulsans to support local businesses and nonprofits. With the City of Tulsa backing the effort, TulsaResponds became the hub for pandemic support. It started strong, with over seven hundred inquiries and responses in the first week, and built from there. It became a lifeline.

"We were very fortunate to have an intern like McKenna, who, rather than seek approval, just launched TulsaResponds on her own," Michael told us for our 2021 playbook. "We believe leadership can come from anywhere, and I'd encourage other cities to seek solutions from everyone, even those you might not expect." He was proud of the nimble nature of the plan, a "building the plane while flying it" effort to rescue the wider community.

"FDR said, 'The test of our progress is not whether we add more to the abundance of those who have much; it is whether we provide enough for those who have too little,'" Michael said. "But COVID not only ground our job creation efforts to a halt, it threatened hundreds of independent businesses that make Tulsa a vibrant city. In that moment launching TulsaResponds became the sole focus for much of the team because we wanted to do everything in our power to save these businesses and the jobs they provide."

ELEVEN

The Great Unbundling

At the beginning of 2020, Rise of the Rest was actively planning for our next tour when we came crashing down to earth with the arrival of a global pandemic.

Revolution's offices, like most others across the country, were empty. From our homes we instituted remote operations and talked about when we'd get back to normal. But before long I came to see there would be no getting back to normal, at least not the way things used to be. It became clear to me that this was a shake-the-snow-globe moment. Everything was upended in an instant, and life and work would never be the same.

My wife, Jean, and I spent much of 2020 on our farm in Warrenton, Virginia, about an hour outside of Revolution's DC headquarters. Like many, it took us a while to come to terms with the pandemic, and the speed at which it was upending lives. We watched as our over-scheduled calendars quickly became empty, as events (including our planned ninth Rise of the Rest bus tour) got canceled or postponed.

The full cost of the pandemic, measured in loss of human

life and extreme suffering for millions of people around the world, is still difficult to calculate. But we're able to look ahead and see some hopeful trends emerging from all the suffering.

There are megatrends that were brewing before the pandemic but which definitely have accelerated. One megatrend is the "Great Resignation"—people leaving their jobs, often to upgrade to better opportunities. The pandemic also led to a *great rethinking*—what the role of companies should be, increasing the importance of investing in resilient supply chains and a broad range of sustainable businesses. People are hungry to bring new meaning to what they do, and to be empowered by their work. Young people in particular feel the importance of working for companies that "stand for something."

The changes are not just around commerce and convenience, and they're not superficial. The deeper question has arisen: How and where will we work and live? Every organization and individual is grappling with that right now.

Perhaps one of the most perceptive comments was made by Virginia senator Tim Kaine, who said, "In the twentieth century, talent served capital. In the twenty-first century, capital will serve talent."

A Hybrid Future

In April 2020, Airbnb CEO Brian Chesky had every reason to fear his business model was crashing. By its nature, Airbnb was reliant on the travel industry, so common sense would tell you that the company was endangered. The numbers seemed to signal a collapse. Most bookings were canceled, and the company had to quickly scale back its costs and ambitions.

But Brian had weathered many storms in Airbnb's young

history, and he immediately started thinking about how the company could pivot. He didn't sink into fear or denial. Early on he acknowledged publicly, "Travel as we know it is over." If that was the case, what did it mean for Airbnb? With their traditional short-term rentals off the table for the foreseeable future, he started to focus on longer-term bookings, appealing to those who wanted to "work from home" wherever they chose—including a favorite getaway. At the same time Brian took care of his core business and the people he relied on most—hosts who rented their homes. He set aside $250 million to reimburse them for lost bookings, and to help them stay in business. By late 2020 he was confident, even bullish, about Airbnb's future and took the company public, in a popular IPO that valued Airbnb at more than $50 billion.

During the pandemic Brian discovered that his travel business model was expanding to something far greater. Now, not only were people vacationing in Airbnbs, they were living and working in them.

Because he's been at the forefront of so many work/life trends, Brian was the perfect person to invite to share a stage with me at the virtual Rise of the Rest Tech Talent Tour in June 2021. We organized this tour as a major event for entrepreneurs, at a time when everybody was trying to figure out what the short- and long-term impacts of the pandemic might be, including on hiring and retaining talent. More than 1,600 people signed up to participate, 25 percent of whom were attendees from California and New York who were thinking about moving to other places. More than one thousand jobs from one hundred companies in fifty cities were on display, pitching both companies and cities. The timing of this Talent Tour, including what in essence was a job fair for startups in rising cities, proved to be ideal. It was clear that people were beginning to rethink the landscape, and their interests were reinforcing the fundamental idea of Rise of the Rest.

By this time, Rise of the Rest had physically visited forty-three cities and made investments in over one hundred. We'd seen tremendous promise. So, the question on our minds was how to harness the moment, and turn it into a movement.

"It's hard to design a post-pandemic world in the middle of a pandemic," Brian said, a point well taken. But we both took a shot at envisioning some possibilities and some general principles.

"I am on the side of more flexibility," Brian told me, predicting that in general tech companies would move toward more flexible working environments. "I think the future is significantly more remote than anyone's getting credit for. And my prediction, early in the pandemic, was big tech companies and other tech companies were going to roll out these hybrid models that were going to be not that flexible, and that over time employees would push back—and the employees, not the companies, would ultimately determine the policies, because it's such a competitive market."

That made sense to me. The battle for talent—attracting and keeping the best people—would be a priority, and that would necessitate flexibility, including supporting remote work long after the pandemic subsided. Going in, most didn't think video-conferencing would work very well, but once people were forced to use it, and everybody was on the same level—in boxes on a Zoom screen—they realized it did allow for collaboration, with an added level of convenience and flexibility.

But I wondered how companies would adjust to a post-pandemic world, where some are in the office and others are working from home. It's likely to be much trickier in terms of team dynamics, company cultures, and trust. Some worry that when things go back, those who continue to work remotely will suffer major FOMO—fear of missing out. As in the hit play *Hamilton*, people may feel left out if they're not in the "room where it happens," which is still likelier to be a physical conference room, or perhaps a discussion in the hall or at the coffee machine. Company cultures will need to change to accommodate these new hybrid work scenarios, and we don't quite know how that will go.

In spite of the challenges, Brian's optimism about this new way of work was very high. "I'll give a plug to Atlanta because we're opening a technology hub in Atlanta," he said. "It's a place with great universities. It's a very diverse city and we're having a lot of success finding really good talent in Atlanta. So, we created an East Coast technical hub in Atlanta. I think it's a great city. I don't think Silicon Valley will ever get re-created, and I don't think Silicon Valley will ever quite be what it was, because I think the whole point is you'll never need to be in one place quite like you used to. It doesn't mean there won't be benefits to all being in a great place. It doesn't mean there won't be the same clusters of people. It's just that this is the worst video technology will ever be ever again, right? It's only going to be better. Bandwidth's going to improve, screen technology is going to improve. We're going to have more tools for connection. It's going to get even easier." He believes that as the technology becomes more seamless, workers are going to have more options to live where they want.

When I mentioned my prediction that there would be dozens of tech hub cities in the United States, not just a few more, Brian laughed. "I had in my head *hundreds* of cities, maybe, and I'm thinking around the world. So, I think it's going to be extremely distributed. The place to be will be the internet. You can access it anywhere."

The workforce seems to be more adaptable than anyone would have expected, and people have quickly grown more comfortable with a hybrid structure. When companies were first forced to operate remotely, there were many real fears that employees would be unable to be productive from home, and that communications would falter. But most people were pleasantly surprised by how well the remote alternative worked. It put an end to the long-held myth that workers had to be physically present to fully engage in their jobs. For their part, many workers have discovered new freedom and lifestyle benefits from remote work.

That's not to say that remote work is a panacea. Long before the pandemic, companies were struggling with how to provide a work/life balance for their employees. This affected women employees the most. Even when companies had generous family-leave policies, women suffered for not being physically present in the office. When remote work became the norm during the pandemic, with many companies promising to continue some form of it, there was an automatic assumption that this would help resolve the persistent juggling problems of working moms. Workers soon learned what anyone with small children instinctively knows—you can't really work at home when small children are clamoring for your attention. Instead of being better for women, the workforce lost as many as two million women during the pandemic. Being home did not "solve" the childcare issues; it often only exacerbated them. Burnout was high. And as companies return to the office, there are real concerns that hybrid models may favor young single people over families and people with children.

Beyond Silicon Valley

We have seen encouraging data points that give us a sense of how the changes are taking shape. The first is the acceleration of funding to early-stage startups outside of the Bay Area and the acceleration of remote work opportunities in tech. "Beyond Silicon Valley," our joint report with PitchBook, got a lot of press attention when it was released in late 2021. Most industry observers were surprised by the data, which showed a dramatic acceleration in venture capital flowing to Rise of the Rest cities.

There were two numbers in particular that caught even my attention. The first was that more than 1,400 new regional venture capital firms had been started in the past ten years, which bodes well for the startups in rising cities. And the second was that venture dollars had increased 600 percent since 2011, from $4 billion to $24 billion in these long-neglected cities.

Those numbers were striking, as they added quantitative specificity to the qualitative arguments we'd been making for years. But that wasn't the only research report that highlighted the transformation taking place. Before the pandemic, less than 10 percent of the American labor force worked remotely full-time. Early in the pandemic, that number jumped to nearly 50 percent. Pew Research predicts that when everything has opened up, the percentage of fully remote workers could remain as high as 25 percent. Our survey of companies in the Rise of the Rest Seed Fund portfolio indicates that those long-term numbers might be even higher in tech. As noted earlier, before the pandemic, only 20 percent of the companies we had backed had remote work options; more than 70 percent of respondents now say they plan to keep remote work policies largely intact.

The COVID-induced acceleration of these trends around

capital and talent may usher in "the great unbundling" of work and life. Historically, where you work and where you live have been a package deal, but the remote work revolution is changing that and allowing companies to compete for talent on different terms. Venture investors pay close attention to the innovation that emerges when startups unbundle the offerings of industry incumbents. The same thing is happening with startup talent recruitment. Startups, no longer wed to the long-standing work/life bundle, can better compete for talent on the basis of the vision, mission, and potential impact of their business. And cities all across the country can now directly market quality of life to people open to relocation. As Brian Chesky said, cities are now competing, and the customers are new residents. One example is Tulsa Remote, a pay-to-relocate program that offered $10,000, free desk space at a coworking center, and a supportive community for those moving to the city within a twelve-month time frame. More than 1,300 people took them up on it.

While many cities are enjoying an increase in job postings, there are clear winners and losers. The data still shows that people tend to be moving from expensive to less expensive and from dense to less dense markets. If people can work anywhere, that puts pressure on more expensive cities to make life more affordable and livable, or they risk losing the talent race.

Our real estate team at Revolution predicts that three types of geographies are poised to be winners in the Great Reshuffle:

1. Affordable, dynamic, midsize cities such as Huntsville and Raleigh. These areas were doing very well pre-pandemic and are now poised to accelerate.
2. "Zoom towns" such as Bozeman and Burlington. These

areas offer tremendous amenities but were often thought of as seasonal or vacation spots before the world of remote work.

3. Super-commuter neighborhoods outside of larger cities such as Chicago and Dallas, that would have been too far for a daily commute, but are fine for an occasional commute.

Along with these configurations, we're spotting some livability trends that will factor into the talent race. For example, a great music scene. It's no coincidence that Nashville and Austin are booming and are music cities. Another factor is a sense of community. The Atlanta BeltLine and the coming Brickline in St. Louis offer experiences to walk, run, and bike to different points of the city. These efforts score very high on the livability scale. Combined with thriving job-creating startup ecosystems, these types of amenities could make the difference.

A Startup Cracks the Recruitment Code

Jacob (Jake) Hsu never imagined that he'd be living and working in Baltimore. He was a Silicon Valley guy through and through, an immigrant success story who had come from Taiwan as a child and was founding startups in San Mateo. His most recent startup, Symbio, a product development and outsourcing service company, had been acquired for over a billion dollars in 2016, and Jake was looking for his next challenge when he heard about Catalyte.

Catalyte was the creation of Michael Rosenbaum, a Harvard economics and law fellow who had once advised the Clinton White House. Rosenbaum was focused on one of the great challenges tech companies face—finding top talent. He felt the standard methods had grown obsolete. Rosenbaum became convinced that potential talent was being overlooked by a system that valued pedigree over innate ability. He believed the talent was out there, but often being missed, and, as a result, opportunity wasn't being evenly distributed. He came up with the idea of ignoring the typical résumé points and instead matching prospective employees according to their abilities and potential, which would be determined through carefully calibrated metrics and AI design.

Rosenbaum bet heavily on his premise, founding Catalyte. And he chose to launch his startup in Baltimore, a post-industrial city abandoned by its undergirding industries, which would serve as the ideal test for his theory.

More than a century earlier, Baltimore had been a bustling center of shipbuilding and trade, and then steel. The Sparrows Point area of the city once housed a Bethlehem Steel plant that was the largest in the world. Opened in 1889, the plant was shaken when Bethlehem Steel declared bankruptcy in 2001. It finally closed in 2012.

The departure of industries left Baltimore with a large, dislocated population of workers who were not connected to the future job opportunities. Rosenbaum's premise was that among these workers, some might emerge as the city's tech engineers of tomorrow. He set about building a model to identify candidates who had the innate ability to learn software engineering, if they were inspired and given the chance. He then provided training, including apprenticeships, and then put the newly minted engineers to work on projects.

Jake first heard about Catalyte from another investor. The way he described it, "It was like Moneyball for software engineering." Moneyball, of course, was the famed baseball strategy memorialized in Michael Lewis's best-selling book and then in a movie starring Brad Pitt, which held that you could predict performance by evaluating results and working backward to form winning teams, even though the data-driven selections could seem counterintuitive.

Curious, Jake decided to make a trip to Baltimore to see for himself. He was skeptical that the method would work. "Within minutes of walking through the door, I had my head totally spun around about this technology and the business," he told us.

The first thing that struck him was the diversity of the apprentices. "This was an engineering team that looked like no other engineering team I'd ever seen," he said. "This team looked like Baltimore. A third of the engineers were Black developers. A third of the engineers were female developers. Half the workforce didn't have a college degree." It was a revelation. And his respect deepened when he saw the performance results, which were off the charts, even with highly complex tasks. The teams were delivering fast, with high-quality results, and doing it cost-effectively.

Jake also noticed that the compensation was making a substantial difference to the workers, who went from earning an average of $25,000 a year in their previous jobs to around $100,000 a year once they'd been trained by Catalyte. This was a dramatic increase for a population of non–college grads, which underscored Catalyte's mission of opening up real opportunity to those who had been left behind. Take the requirement for a college degree out of the equation and focus on the underlying talent, and anything was possible.

Jake flew back to Silicon Valley, his mind spinning. "I couldn't let go of this idea that here was an opportunity to use technology to unleash the potential of people. You could literally take people in any location, any demographic, regardless of their credentials and background, and identify those who could become great software engineers."

He decided to invest in Catalyte in 2016. Two months later, the presidential election happened, and "the world got turned upside down." Jake looked around at the echo chamber of the Silicon Valley tech world and had a wakeup call: "We couldn't keep growing our economy by leaving half the workforce behind," he said. "The pedigree bias had been exacerbating the opportunity gap, the wealth gap, and the skills gap. It was a self-perpetuating vicious cycle." Jake defined pedigree in the tech world as not just referring to educational degrees, prior employment, upbringing, and contacts. At a more macro level it's the presumption that tech talent can only be found in California, Boston, and New York. He was determined to be a part of the solution, and within months he had relocated to Baltimore and stepped into the role of CEO of Catalyte.

In 2018, Catalyte became one of Rise of the Rest Seed Fund's initial investments in our first $150 million seed fund. We saw the potential in the technology and use of AI, which would extend opportunities for those who were previously left out of the tech world. And we were especially attracted to Catalyte's commitment to Baltimore and other postindustrial cities.

The pandemic brought a special opportunity for Catalyte to demonstrate its feasibility in a large collaboration with the city of Baltimore. Baltimore desperately needed to upgrade its IT infrastructure, but the cost of consultants and engineers was prohibitive. Catalyte built a model showing that, for the cost of the city's two current consultants, it could deliver a team of a dozen locally trained software developers. The team quickly went to work updating the city's digital services. Then came the special pandemic need of contact tracing. Catalyte took the same team of a dozen people and rapidly upskilled them to build contact tracing applications. Again, they performed beautifully. Then came the need to build a vaccine reservation system. Catalyte further upskilled the team and set them to work.

As Jake described it, the effort proved two things to Baltimore. First, that Catalyte could save the city money, by being much more efficient and productive. The second innovation was using the same team—so now the city had a trusted team who understood how the city worked. Above all that, one of the bonuses was that Catalyte was creating a pipeline of talent for the city—and also an opportunity. As the pandemic waned, city officials began consulting with Catalyte on how it could continue to retrain its existing employees so they would not be displaced.

Is a Talent Boomerang Real?

I'd been discussing the notion of a talent boomerang for a few years. Admittedly, it was not just a prediction based on facts; it was also an aspiration based on hope. Where once those who graduated from colleges in their states might leave the area for careers on the coasts or to pursue tech dreams in Silicon Valley, now some were returning home. This trend was especially occurring among millennials, who were moving home in large numbers, often because of cost of living and quality of life concerns.

Communities were already vying to become places that would attract tech talent. But on a larger scale, COVID opened up a national conversation about coming home. This happened first of all because people were actually moving back in with parents or leaving cities to live in less dense or more desirable settings during the pandemic. Much of this was temporary, but still highlighted the desire to be someplace else, if that was an option—which it was, in a remote world.

People were also gravitating to more sustainable lifestyles. With rising housing and living costs in coastal cities like San Francisco, the pandemic seemed to initially accelerate a movement of people away from the coastal tech hubs.

In addition to changing location, people were also thinking of changing jobs. According to Prudential's Pulse of the American Worker Survey, one in four workers planned to look for a job at a different company once the pandemic has subsided.

In the past, a lot of people decided what kind of work they wanted to do, and that determined the rest of the decisions in their lives, including where they lived. The ultimate purpose of Rise of the Rest was to generate startup cultures throughout the country. Now, because of the pandemic, I think we can accelerate the dispersion of talent—or really the boomerang of talent, since many are returning to places where they grew up or went to school.

One question is, if people move, where are they going to live? The stagnant models for housing—buy a house or rent for a minimum of twelve months, with large upfront expenditures for down payments and security deposits—seem designed for another era. Most of this housing has been built with yesterday's worker in mind. There is also a lack of housing that has the correct amenities, flexibility, and technology for people to work from home.

In our conversation for the Tech Talent Tour, Brian Chesky

observed, "Cities are going to have to compete for talent. And I think the cities that win will be the cities that most welcome talent. In a world with more mobility, it's actually easier [to attract talent]. Even with Airbnb, you can get a house for three months. You don't need to sign a lease. You don't need a first month's rent. You don't need to put down a deposit. You can uproot pretty quickly. And so people have a lot more choice." And, he pointed out, cities are communicating, "Hey, we're open for business. We'd love to have you here."

The influential tech podcast *All-In* reported on the dramatic shift that had taken place during the pandemic, noting that states like Florida, Texas, Arizona, North Carolina, South Carolina, and Tennessee had seen dramatic jumps in people moving there, while other states saw declines, including California, New York, Illinois, and Massachusetts. Asked to name the biggest trend he was seeing heading into 2022, *All-In* cohost David Sacks, a successful entrepreneur and investor, answered, "Rise of the Rest. I think it's a trend that's been going on but it's going to keep getting bigger next year."

A Founder Takes on the Hiring Void

Jamie Baxter figures he's been an entrepreneur all his life, even when he worked in corporate America. So, when Chris Loeffler, a hotel owner, described his struggles staffing hotels, with a 100 percent turnover every year and daily no-shows, Jamie thought that was a problem an entrepreneur should tackle. He considered it for a couple of years, focusing on a simple idea: what if managers and owners like Chris could order staff on their phones like they'd order an Uber? Push a few buttons and, like magic, people would show up to work.

Jamie had experience in recruiting and performance management and in finding and placing talent, so this was in his wheelhouse. He asked Chris if he'd be interested in tackling this project with him and using his hotels as an incubator. They began with a thorough analysis of the staffing issue. The hotels relied on staffing agencies, but they constantly ran into problems because they could never hire enough people to accommodate special occasions. If they had a big event, they might call for twenty extra bartenders. Not only did the agencies charge sky-high prices but they were very unreliable. "Maybe ten bartenders would actually show up," he said. "If it was a really good day, maybe six of them actually knew how to pour a drink and the others were just warm bodies." If there was a tight schedule, it was impossible. "They couldn't do technology. They had one staffing agency that was actually faxing forms to tell them what they needed. I thought, 'Okay, there's a whole lot of room for improvement here.'"

Jamie's next step was to test the market. How many people out there would respond to job calls through an app? He advertised as if a job already existed, and when people responded he ran them through a quick survey and gave them a $20 Amazon gift card for their trouble. They collected data this way and then built a website. After that they built a web form on the business side and ran the plan manually for a while, actually sending out text messages to potential workers: "Hey Joe, we have a job at the Hyatt, downtown Phoenix paying $20 an hour on Saturday 6:00 PM. You want to work? Reply yes or no."

The testing went well enough to plan for a launch. They named the startup Qwick. The sophistication and the effectiveness of the system happened when the Qwick app was perfected. When potential workers sign up, they start by giving their experience, and based on that the app will go through twenty questions about bartending, waiting, dishwashing, or whatever the skill might be. Once candidates pass the quiz, they're invited to an orientation, also through the app, which includes a video interview. That's the initial vetting. Next comes details such as making sure applicants have the right certifications, and then there's a fourteen-point Qwick certification. After that, applicants are ready to accept shifts.

However, much like the Uber rating system, vetting is an ongoing process.

"When you get out of an Uber, you rate the driver," Jamie said. "With Qwick, you work a shift, and the business will rate you, but we also know that you showed up on time."

Once the app was up and running, Qwick took off. Workers loved the independence of it, plus the immediate paycheck. Businesses loved the reliability and flexibility of an on-demand workforce.

Then the pandemic struck. "We had made what turned out not to be a great decision, to push our fundraise from the fall of 2019 to the spring of 2020," Jamie said. "Our revenue dropped, and no one would fund us. We ended up having to lay off seventy percent of the team. We went from fifty-four people down to nineteen. Ultimately, our existing investors, including Rise of the Rest, stepped up and put some more money in, so we could live another day. We slowly came out of 2020, and we actually ended up beating revenue over 2019 by a hair. I'll call that a win every day, given the pandemic."

Once the pandemic shutdowns had lifted, it was a dramatically different story. Now the employment crunch was at a crisis level. "Suddenly the whole world was talking about the dissatisfaction of workers and the need for something to change—exactly what we'd based our business on."

Four years in, Jamie is grateful his company is "mature" enough to capitalize on what he calls the "epic timing" of being at the center of a groundbreaking generational shift in how we work.

Immigration: America's Innovation Weapon

On February 13, 2013, the year before I launched Rise of the Rest, I was called upon to testify before a Senate Judiciary Committee hearing on Comprehensive Immigration Reform. Reflecting back on my testimony, I feel the frustration that so much of our progress on immigration has been derailed in recent years. At the time I reminded the senators of something that still bears repeating today—that America did not become great by luck or accident. It was the work of pioneering entrepreneurs—beginning with the country's earliest settlers, our nation's first immigrant entrepreneurs, who took a risk hoping to turn dreams into businesses. From the Mom and Pop bakery on Main Street to fast-growing tech companies like PayPal, the primary drivers of our economic growth have been and will continue to be startup businesses that create value, generate revenue, produce jobs, spur innovation, and expand the tax base. I emphasized that high-skilled immigrants have always been job creators, not job takers. According to a Kauffman Foundation study, one-fourth of US-based startups were launched by foreign-born founders; in Silicon Valley, that number is closer to 50 percent.

I concluded my testimony with what I hoped was a wakeup call. "What distinguishes us is that we have always been a magnet for risk-taking men and women from across the world hoping to start businesses, innovate, and contribute," I told the senators. "That is part of our DNA. It is why in the twentieth century we created more wealth, opportunity, and economic growth than any other nation." But I cautioned that the advantage was slipping away. As we made it increasingly difficult to settle in the United States, other countries were stepping up. The world doesn't stand still.

As everyone knows by now, comprehensive immigration reform did not pass Congress then, or at any point since. As I write this, we have a new opportunity to get it right, and I hope we take it. History teaches us that progress belongs to countries that are open, and that has always been America's edge.

According to a TechNet report, the issue has been even more urgent, with 64 percent of American employers reporting concerns over a skills gap, and stating that expanding high-skilled immigration is the best solution.

New American Economy (NAE) released a report in 2021 demonstrating the contribution of immigrants in one hundred of America's largest cities—home to almost 85 percent of all immigrants. The big takeaway: immigrants are responsible for more than half of all growth in nineteen metro areas, including some of the largest in the country, such as Dallas, Las Vegas, and Raleigh. Overall, immigrants in the largest one hundred metro areas were major drivers of local economies, earning more than $1.5 trillion in 2019 alone. This allowed them to contribute more than $439.6 billion in state and local taxes and hold almost $1.1 trillion in consumer spending power.

The growth trends are interesting. Although the most immigrant-dense metro area was Miami, where almost 42 percent of the population was not born in the United States, there were other notable cities. The report cited the Dallas-Fort Worth metro area, which added more than 48,000 new immigrant residents in one year, making it the fastest-growing metro area for immigrants. It also cited San Jose, Austin, Charlotte, Raleigh, and Atlanta.

It's just a fact; we cannot keep our entrepreneurial edge in the world if we do not welcome entrepreneurs to our country. We need this infusion of talent in order to succeed. The global battle for talent is real, and it's fierce. We want the best talent to come here, as they have in the past. The question is: will we be able to make it happen? Our future depends on it.

If you clear away all the political vitriol aimed at immigrants, the facts are, as Ronald Reagan (a supporter of immigration) would say, "stubborn things." According to *Forbes*, immigrant entrepreneurs start 25 percent of all new businesses in the United States. An MIT Sloan study found that those new businesses create 42 percent more jobs than those started by US-born entrepreneurs.

I've had the chance to meet dozens of extraordinary immigrant entrepreneurs over the years. One of them, Hamdi Ulukaya, the founder of Chobani, landed in New York at the age of twenty-three with little more than hope. He ended up buying a shuttered Kraft Foods plant in upstate New York and set out to perfect a recipe for Greek yogurt. He went from five employees to more than two thousand as Chobani became the number one yogurt brand in the United States. Hamdi was so grateful that he gave equity to every single Chobani employee, so they could all share in the company's success. Hamdi has gone on to inspire a new generation of entrepreneurs, including with the launch of the Chobani Food Incubator, to support food entrepreneurs aiming to challenge the industry and bring better food to more people. I had the pleasure of serving alongside him as fellow Presidential Ambassadors for Global Entrepreneurship.

Daniel Lubetzky, the founder of KIND Snacks, was born in Latvia and raised in Lithuania. His father was a Holocaust survivor, having been a young boy in the Dachau concentration camp. Daniel learned at an early age the importance of kindness and empathy, and after his family immigrated to San Antonio, Texas, set out to make his mark in the world. Initially he thought he could make the biggest contribution as a diplomat so he went to law school, but after a few years he concluded that business could be the most significant force for societal change. His first company, PeaceWorks, made food products in partnership with Palestinians, Israelis, Jordanians, Egyptians, and Turks. He then followed that with KIND Snacks, which now generates more than $1 billion in annual sales. More recently, I've had the opportunity to brainstorm with Daniel on his new initiatives to promote civility and peace, as he takes the wealth accumulated through his business success and redirects it to have a positive impact on society.

These are two of just the many immigrant stories I've heard, examples of people who have pursued the American Dream, and in the process given thousands of fellow Americans a better life.

TWELVE

The Diversity Imperative

When we go into a new community, we always begin by identifying community champions and asking them to connect us with the people they think we should meet. When we first started doing this, we often ended up sitting at tables that were comprised largely (and occasionally entirely) of white men. There was little diversity.

I guess that shouldn't have surprised us. Only 1 percent of venture capital goes to Black founders and less than 10 percent to women. So, statistically, they're going to be underrepresented. We have seen the benefits of having diversity in our leadership teams at Revolution as well. Diverse investors identify diverse founders, and over time there's a multiplying effect, as founders introduce us to the people in their networks.

In 2019 Rodney Sampson published a paper with his colleague Dell Gines, who works for the Federal Reserve Bank of Kansas City, whose focus is entrepreneur-led development. The paper, "Building Racial Equity in Tech Ecosystems to Spur Local Recovery," was a blueprint for how to ensure that everyone in America is equitably positioned to prosper from the technology-fueled growth of the fourth industrial revolution, especially how communities with little preexisting wealth can build multigenerational wealth.

Rodney and Dell viewed the development of inclusive local tech ecosystems, which are the drivers of Black entrepreneurship, as a step toward solving the nation's racial wealth gap. By prioritizing inclusive tech ecosystems and increasing the Black tech workforce, they envision an improved ability for Black households to leverage the power of innovation to improve local economies and quality of life.

A central feature of their analysis was the Economic Development Pyramid, which is a way of organizing the entrepreneur's journey into the ecosystem—specifically, how to build a network of relationships where one had not existed before. "People cannot aspire to what they're not exposed to," Rodney said. As he explained it, "Historically speaking, African Americans have either been looked at as a productive asset, like a person in the labor market, or just left out altogether. Our question should be: How do we develop these strong, robust entrepreneurship ecosystems so that African Americans and other people of color can participate in the growth of the economy, not just as a productive resource in terms of being in the labor market, but actually the people who are producing innovation and economic growth? For this nation's economy to grow, we've got to be on that innovation, that technology, that productive side of entrepreneurship, because that's where growth comes from, and that's where racial wealth equity comes from too."

The pyramid took people through every stage of development. The bottom level was early exposure and socialization.

Above that was education and skills development. Above that was talent placement, in an internship or apprenticeship. These three levels formed the crucial activity of talent development. The middle levels of the pyramid were new venture development, including innovation, entrepreneurship and market, and capital access. The top line of the pyramid was wealth and job creation.

"We believe that if a person—in this context, a Black person—participates at all levels of that ecosystem, that is the most comprehensive way of closing the racial wealth gap in an individual's life, a family's life, and then a community's life," Rodney said.

A Catalyzing Moment

During the summer of 2020, Rodney and I spoke about the slow progress of equity for Black founders. The numbers were discouraging. In the twenty years since Rodney had begun his work, the number of Black founders had not grown that much, and it still comprised little more than 1 percent of venture dollars. We wanted to figure out how we could step up those efforts, especially during a time when COVID was keeping us off the road. We knew that you don't go from 1 percent Black founders to more equity without taking some extraordinary measures. It's not just something that's going to happen overnight organically.

A renewed focus on racial justice was having a catalyzing effect on the corporate and investment worlds. The societal unrest caused by too many acts of unjust policing against men and women of color demanded that we do more. The movement of Black Lives Matter, which swept across the nation, called out for meaningful action. This was a significant cultural moment, signaling a focus on the need for more inclusivity, including in our arena of entrepreneurship and venture capital.

We realized that we should leverage our Rise of the Rest platform and be more explicit about leveling the playing field not just in terms of place but also in terms of people, with an initial focus on showcasing and investing in Black founders. Not only was the moment rich with opportunity in the Black community but the pandemic forced us to do everything virtually, creating the opportunity to go beyond our usual city-based, bus-centric approach, and do a fully remote tour. Like many aspects of the pandemic, it led us to reimagine how to create events that weren't physical, knowing that the virtual approach would allow us to cast a wider net for founders and investors.

We decided to create a virtual event with Black founders. We received applications from all over the country, and we held a virtual pitch competition. In the end, we invested in six companies, and we partnered with venture capitalists nationwide who agreed to senior-level meetings with the entrepreneurs.

There are a growing number of investors who do want to do better. They do want to be more inclusive. They recognize they have a role to play and want to be part of the solution, not part of the problem. But they often tell us they don't know what to do, as they lack the networks to source startups led by diverse founders.

On the other side, a lot of promising Black founders don't have access to investors. They have great ideas, but don't have the money—or the friends and family with capital to invest—to do that initial seed round.

We announced an ambitious plan for the Rise of the Rest Virtual Tour: Equity Edition, cosponsored by OHUB, along with Morgan Stanley's Multicultural Innovation Hub and the 100 Black Angels & Allies Fund. It would be a virtual week of programming anchored by a $2 million investment pitch competition and a commitment to connect select Black founders with well-known investors from across the country. In addition to receiving seed investments, pitch competition winners would have access to Morgan Stanley's Multicultural Innovation Lab, a five-month intensive accelerator.

In our jointly signed announcement, we wrote:

> We call on everyone in the startup community to commit more resources and capital to ensure that the future of entrepreneurship is an inclusive one. It is our hope that the Equity Edition will serve as a powerful example of how an ecosystem centered in racial equity can operate and benefit us all.
>
> We certainly acknowledge this event we're doing is not going to solve the huge disparity in funding, but it's a step in the right direction. It builds on some of the work we've been doing for five or six years. Funding is important. Ultimately investing, writing checks is a big part of it. But the most lasting is to be part of a broader network. That's what we've done with Rise of the Rest.

The construct of the virtual tour was going to be a little different than usual: ten semifinalists, five finalists, and three winners. The first-place winner would receive $1 million, and two runners-up would receive $500,000 each, from a mix of investors including Revolution, Morgan Stanley, and the 100 Black Angels & Allies Fund. In addition, the winners would have other benefits, because while money is important, for us this was mostly about connectivity and opening doors to opportunities. The winners would be invited to join the

Morgan Stanley Multicultural Innovation Lab—a five-month accelerator—receive personal meetings with at least five venture capitalists, and receive pitch support and reviews from our team of investors and entrepreneurs. Nearly five hundred Black-led startups applied, representing a broad array of industries. The range was impressive, and we were proud to play a role in amplifying their stories.

Among the most meaningful aspects of the virtual tour were the segments where entrepreneurial leaders and investors participated in panel discussions to offer guidance to entrepreneurs. I hosted one of these panels with Aaron Walker, founder and CEO of Camelback Ventures, which is dedicated to increasing access to opportunity for entrepreneurs of color and women by investing in their ventures and leadership while advocating for fairness in their funding; and Shelly Bell, founder and CEO of Black Girl Ventures, which is dedicated to providing access to capital for Black and Brown women entrepreneurs.

Aaron pointed out that inclusion in investing in entrepreneurs is a matter of choice. There's no secret formula. "The talent is already there," he said. "And I think that what we've just chosen to do is to recognize that talent and go looking for it and say that it doesn't have to look the same. It doesn't have to go to the same school, look the same way, talk the same way."

We were all aware, in the midst of the pandemic, that the "norm" had disappeared, but Shelly urged us to not return to the norm—to find a new norm.

"How do we not go back to the norm . . . what does the new norm look like?" she posed. "There is something that we can do and we can innovate."

We agreed that we definitely didn't want to go back to the

norm, which didn't work for so many people, including people of color. "We need to do better than normal." And storytelling was a key way we could do that—telling the stories of entrepreneurs and their journeys and the battles they've had to fight. Statistics also matter because they galvanize people and grab their attention.

"The normal prototype of an entrepreneur is typically white, typically male," Aaron said. "But when you look at the data and look at the statistics, the fastest growing group of entrepreneurs over the last ten years are Black women, and a close second are Latina women. So I think when we're talking about entrepreneurs, that should really be the face of entrepreneurship. And we sort of say in this country, 'There are not enough people who want to be entrepreneurs.' I don't think that's as true as we think it is, but there are a lot of people who do want to be entrepreneurs and who are doing it every day. It's just that we don't see them as such. But in fact, they are the fastest growing group of entrepreneurs, and we should be investing in them."

One of the foundational philosophies of Camelback Ventures is to be "ruthless for good." I asked Aaron to talk about that idea. "This concept of ruthless for good came to me a little bit after 2008, right when we were having a great recession," he said. Seeing the ruthlessness in society, "I thought to myself, 'What would it look like if we had that same mentality, that same drive, that same unapologetic nature toward social change?' In many ways, I think that ruthlessness is neutral. It really just depends on how you use it. And what we're focused on at Camelback is how can we use that ethos and that nature to push for equity, to push for the kind of just world that we want to live in."

Shelly added, "After the murder of George Floyd, I saw money move in a way that I've never seen before. People were waking up to realities that they had never woken up to before."

A Founder's Model for Change Starts with Hair Salons

"We are not the traditional founders by any means, whether you look at age, creed, or race," Courtney Caldwell said of the startup ShearShare, which she and her husband, Tye, launched in 2017. "We are two African American founders who are married and who have no technical background. We started ShearShare in the middle of America and are now living and working out of Buffalo, New York. People are like, 'Tech unicorns don't come from McKinney, Texas, or Buffalo.' And we say, 'You wanna see?'"

Courtney exudes passion for her company and for a worker community to which ShearShare is devoted. "I love our story because it is one that really is a model of hope. We're a shining example of the idea that if you're passionate about something you can actually make it work."

She's particularly proud of being married founders—not that common. "I like to say that our marriage is our first startup, and that's a Class A merger. Our son is our second startup and he's been acquired, because he's a junior cadet at the Air Force Academy. And ShearShare is our third startup. Early on, investors would say, 'Oh, I don't know about married cofounders.' And then the next second they'd say, 'Cofounding relationships are like a marriage.' We agreed—'We've got that one covered.'"

Tye had been in the beauty industry for thirty years as a barber and cosmetologist. Courtney had met him in his salon. At the time she worked in full-time ministry but went on to spend the next twenty years in B2B tech marketing. However, she was very close to Tye's work. "When you marry an entrepreneur, you get pulled into the business," she laughed. "His work doesn't stop when he comes home and sits down at the dinner table. Even though I was working for the Oracles of the world, I was always pulled into these conversations around inventory in the salon and barber shop, and hiring, and vendor relationships, and advertising and branding."

But around 2012, just after they expanded the salon to include both open stations and private suites, the industry was starting to change. Suddenly they didn't have a waitlist anymore and were asking, "Where are all the people?" One day Tye got a call from a hairstylist who had moved and needed to be closer to her clientele and wondered if she could rent a station by the day. This was not done in the industry, and they thought it was a fluke—until others started calling. It snowballed into a demand in surrounding communities and became a win-win for both the beauticians and salons. Stylists didn't have to sign long-term contracts and had flexibility; salons were able to fill their empty chairs. They were in the early stages of developing a successful marketplace.

The driving insight was that the loyalty was between the client and the stylist, not between the client and the name on the outside of the brick-and-mortar marquee. Yet, in the process of more directly connecting stylists and clients, ShearShare actually saved many small businesses whose empty chairs were draining their capital.

"We were trying to help other small business owners. We were tired of hearing the stories of our fellow barber shop and salon and spa owners having to shut down because they couldn't get stylists to come in and do the work," Courtney said. "With our business idea we were saying, 'Let's figure this out for everybody's benefit.' We were committed to helping an industry that had fed our family for three decades."

One night Courtney and Tye sat at a table at Chipotle and sketched out the elements of an app on a napkin. Courtney shared it with a contact she'd met through LinkedIn, who began describing to her "this thing called a startup." That contact turned out to be TD Lowe, a Silicon Valley adviser to a range of startups.

There was no question of moving ShearShare to Silicon Valley. Courtney and Tye were determined to grow the business from McKinney, which is about thirty minutes from Dallas. But TD Lowe did introduce them to the idea of startup competitions, and that's where Rise of the Rest connected with ShearShare.

The occasion was the Google Demo Day in March 2018, when eleven startups had the chance to pitch. We'd committed to investing $250,000 in the top two "Judges' Favorites," as well as $150,000 to any of the remaining nine that raised $1 million in the next six months. Courtney shone in her pitch and the judges awarded her the top prize. Rise of the Rest began our relationship with ShearShare, which included additional investments as Courtney and Tye built the business.

Today ShearShare is in nine hundred cities nationwide and managing more than $90 million in salon and barbershop space assets. "Every city or town, even the smallest, has three constants," Courtney noted. "You're always going to find a post office. You're always going to find a place of worship. And you're always going to find a Mom and Pop salon or a neighborhood barbershop. We're everywhere."

Courtney, who was once a full-time minister, imbues her work with a deep sense of purpose and caring—a strong desire to make the world a better place for those she serves. Being a married founder couple and being African American are big parts of that picture. "I tell people that I'm on the best, and the saddest, list ever," Courtney said. "That's the list of the number of Black women who have raised over a million dollars in VC funding for their startup. I'm just number 33. For me, that's a glaring call to do whatever I can to help empower women who have amazing ideas. Sometimes it is as simple as standing up in front of a crowd and saying, 'Hi, my name's Courtney Caldwell. I'm the cofounder of ShearShare.' And that gives people enough umph and gumption to go out there and say, 'You know what? I can do that too.' They can take the leap just as we did. I always say that the entrepreneurial spirit is every day jumping and growing your wings on the way down."

The Big Pitch

The excitement was building for the Rise of the Rest Equity Edition pitch competition, but first we heard from an inspiring speaker. One of the entrepreneurs we brought to our virtual audience was Dr. Lonnie Johnson, a heralded inventor, entrepreneur, and aerospace engineer—and, most famously, the inventor of the Super Soaker, which has been a best-selling toy for decades. Dr. Johnson told a very moving story that was a tribute to his parents, who enabled him from an early age. In grade school they knew he wanted to be an engineer, although he didn't have the word for it. He called it designing things and building things. He built a robot in his mother's kitchen, taking up one-third of the space for rocket parts and tools. One day he was mixing rocket fuel when it went off, sending smoke billowing everywhere and burning holes in the table and chairs. When his dad came home from work, he said, "You're going to have to do that outside." His parents gave him a hot plate and he continued his project. There was no punishment, no discouragement. He never forgot that incident and how much it meant to him to have his parents' calm, steady encouragement.

Building a Company to Advance the Circular Economy

The winner of the $1 million pitch competition was Chicago-based Rheaply, a resource exchange platform that allows resources to be reused, creating a more connected, circular economy. The founder, Dr. Garry Cooper, started his entrepreneurial journey while working at his lab at Northwestern University in Chicago, where he was doing a PhD in neural science, trying to find a cure for Parkinson's disease. From time to time, his colleagues from other labs would mention that they wished they had a particular piece of equipment or a certain chemical. If he had extras of what they needed in his lab, he'd pass it on to them. "Labs have lots of materials, lots of stuff," he said, adding that it is often super pricey. Being chronically underfunded, labs are always scrambling to get supplies. So, Garry started sharing the stuff he no longer needed, piling it onto a cart to distribute to other labs. He didn't ask permission; he just did it. The other labs were grateful; they called him "the cart guy." He compared it to the ice cream man of his youth if he'd been giving away ice cream, not selling it—"Here comes Garry, the ice cream man, with two thousand dollar chemicals."

After he left Northwestern, he was missed. "People would still email me at Northwestern—'Hey Garry, where's the cart?' Or, 'You got this? You got that?' And I'm like, 'I've not been there for three years.' So that's kind of the birth of Rheaply, asking how we can build a technology or a system that survives a single point of failure, like me and the cart, and then is more robust." Garry's best friend was a web developer and Garry had often pitched him ideas and regularly got a thumbs-down response. But this time his friend said, "You might have something."

Being an entrepreneur had never occurred to Garry. "In some ways I think it felt a little bit untouchable," he admitted. "I thought, 'Oh, my gosh. Steve Jobs is an entrepreneur. I'm just Garry from Dayton.'" He also noted that he came up in a scientific community where the overarching momentum was to become faculty members or research scientists, not to be thinking about business and creating companies. Nor did Garry see entrepreneurs in his neighborhood or family. It was a foreign idea. Even so, he grabbed the ring and went for it.

Garry launched Rheaply in November 2016, and he didn't fully realize how rapidly the sustainability movement would gain momentum and how quickly people would embrace the idea of reuse. "The cherry on top was this concept of less waste, less carbon, more efficiency. And today the momentum for net zero is strong. If we're going to get to net zero, what have we got to do? We got to do our renewables. We got to do transport. We've got to solve waste and resource efficiency in the circular economy."

As of this writing, Rheaply has helped its customers divert over fifteen metric tons of waste from landfills—and that's just for platform-related transactions where waste diversion metrics are being tracked by individual users. The company is not only helping its customers be more sustainable but is creating greater opportunities for B2B or business-to-nonprofit resource connectivity within local communities. Today, city governments in places such as San Francisco are investing in the Rheaply platform.

When Garry won the Rise of the Rest pitch competition, he

was overwhelmed by the outpouring of response from Black founders and aspiring Black founders who reached out to him for advice or support. He wondered how he would have the time to take on the task of doing so much. Then he thought of his grandmother. "My grandmother's ninety-five," he said. "She had nineteen children—ten in one marriage, nine in another. She raised all those kids herself. Half of them have advanced degrees. She worked four jobs through their upbringing, and I always think of her and conclude, 'Yeah, I've got a lot of work to do. That's another obligation, but what would my grandmother do?' So, when I think about that and her living through the Depression and Jim Crow and women's suffrage to now, I can't help but be involved in these founders' lives and give whatever I can to bring them into my network."

Paying It Forward

Recalling how difficult it was for her as a Black woman to raise funds, Jewel Burks Solomon, winner of our Atlanta pitch competition, made a vow that if she succeeded, she'd go back and make sure that the experience was better for others coming up. After she sold PartPic to Amazon in 2016, she became the US head of Google for Startups. In 2020 she helped start Collab Capital, with a focus on funding Black entrepreneurs.

Jewel recounted how the evolution of Collab had two chapters. The first was resistance based on the sense that there weren't enough Black entrepreneurs to make it worthwhile. "A lot of people said maybe it was too niche, or there wouldn't be enough of a pipeline and founders for you to vet," Jewel recalled. "We said, no, we're meeting with hundreds of founders that need backing. We were very adamant about sticking to that mission of funding Black founders."

Jewel said that the tune changed after George Floyd's murder. "People were made to see what's going on in this country through the lens of what happened to Floyd. People started to think, okay, maybe we do need to have specific and targeted funds and resources specifically for Black founders. So, our fundraising definitely picked up. That was the tale of the two parts of our fundraise—pre-June of 2020 and post 2020. But at the end of the day, we're really happy that we were able to successfully raise the fund and now have been able to invest in twelve Black-led businesses. We'll invest in fifty over the next three years."

Grateful for her opportunities, and determined to help others realize theirs, Jewel said, "This decade of my life right now is all about equity. It's all about how we make sure that folks, regardless of their backgrounds, have equal access to this industry, which is, in my opinion, the biggest opportunity for wealth generation."

In addition, Jewel noted that her work as head of Google for Startups is also about leveling the playing field for underrepresented founders. She's established programs for Black founders and "we recently announced a fund for Latinx founders. Everything I do at this point is about how to make sure that if a founder has a great idea and they have the right market opportunity and they have all the things that they need to be successful, the resources and access to networks is there."

THIRTEEN

A Sustainable Nation

The most critical challenge for entrepreneurs in the twenty-first century is building the tools for a sustainable world. There's been a significant shift from defining it as a problem to solve, which of course it is, to more of an opportunity to seize.

Nowhere is that question more urgent than in coal country. When people ask, "Is there life after coal?" the response is often somewhere between defeat and defiance. States like West Virginia and Kentucky, where tens of thousands of coal miners have lost well-paying jobs that their families relied on for generations, are left without an obvious path out of the decline.

Jeff Young's book *Appalachian Fall: Dispatches from Coal Country on What's Ailing America* points out that the infrastructure in coal mining communities wasn't developed to support anything but coal, so its decline traumatized the areas. Communities were told to retrain workers, and they rushed to do that, but retrain them for what? "Training a worker for a job doesn't create a job. It really puts the onus on the worker, and suddenly says, 'It's kind of your fault. If only you'd better educate yourself or find a new skill,'" Young says. "It also assumes some mobility on the worker's part to go to wherever this mysterious new job might arise. That has not really worked well for Appalachia."

Yet Young is bullish on a solution to depressed economies flowing through coal country. "In fact, we argue that the resolution to many of America's most pressing challenges lies in better understanding and addressing Appalachia's conundrum," he writes.

One path forward is forged by entrepreneurs who are seeking to turn coal country into a rich agricultural and energy-thriving territory with a twenty-first-century story to tell. One of these entrepreneurs is Jonathan Webb.

When we heard about Jonathan's idea, we were immediately intrigued. Jonathan had a common Kentucky story. His grandmother was raised in Whitley County, where a coal mining accident killed her father, a sad part of his family's legacy. His parents moved to Lexington, where Jonathan grew up seeing the devastating job losses in the region and hearing the stories of those suffering as a result. By the time he was in college at the University of Kentucky, Jonathan knew there wasn't much of a future for him there. When he graduated in 2010—the first in his family to get a college degree—he moved to New York City and found work in the solar power industry. In October 2014, he was hired by the Army Office of Energy Initiatives in Washington, DC, to help the Obama administration achieve its goal of supplying 20 percent of the Department of Defense electricity with renewable energy by 2025.

It was while living in DC and developing sustainable energy farms that Jonathan came across another kind of farming initiative in the Netherlands. There, high-tech greenhouses yielding thirty times more than traditional agriculture and virtually eliminating the use of chemicals were changing the food supply systems in many parts of Europe.

There was nothing like it in the United States, and Jonathan threw himself into researching what it would take to build such a facility on a much larger scale. There was only one place he considered to house that indoor farm: eastern Kentucky. When he'd visit our office, Jonathan was energetic, spreading his binders across our conference table and speaking nonstop as a true evangelist for his plan to feed the world. For him it was a cause with great urgency as, by the year 2050, the world would need 50 to 70 percent more food supply. To achieve that, we'd need alternative sustainable production capabilities such as this large-scale indoor farm network.

It was clear that Jonathan was capitalizing on his personal experience. He was an expert in solar energy, building large solar installations. AppHarvest was a giant construction project too, but instead of energy it was food.

We were intrigued with the idea, even though we knew the execution would be difficult and the company might fail. It was likely a binary situation—it would be either a big success or a total wipeout. It depended on a lot of things coming together in perfect sync: finding the land, getting the approvals, raising the capital, building the physical operation, licensing the technology, and hiring and training the people. The degree of difficulty was admittedly high. However, the potential was great, and we felt it was a battle worth fighting. In addition to our investment, we gave Jonathan support in communications, marketing, and branding his company, doing everything we could to set him up for long-term success.

For his first site Jonathan chose to start with growing to-matoes on a 366-acre former cattle ranch in Morehead, Kentucky, in the eastern part of the state. At 2.7 million square feet, it would be one of the world's largest greenhouses—big enough for more than fifty football fields to fit inside. The location offered a strategic advantage. It was within a day's drive to 70 percent of the US population, so trucks could more efficiently carry the product to the nation. Noting that most tomatoes were shipped from Mexico or California, a five-day drive or more, Jonathan said that his shipping plan would use 80 percent less diesel fuel.

Before Jonathan broke ground, our team traveled to Kentucky to tour the field and attend a high school program hosted by AppHarvest designed to get young people excited about ag-tech. The high school stands were full of skeptical teenagers, but Jonathan ran up onstage like a rock star and enthusiastically spoke about the future of the region. You could see the kids' faces change almost immediately in response to his youthful exuberance. He brought others onstage who were working with AppHarvest to discuss their journey with the company and why students should be excited about farming. "I want to be a high school student in eastern Kentucky right now," he declared, signaling the great things to come.

The students weren't used to thinking that way. Those we talked to shared the familiar tales of job losses, opioid abuse, and how they would have to leave the area after graduation because there was little opportunity. Jonathan was trying to open their eyes to another way, and we could see that contagious hope begin to take hold.

Education was a big part of Jonathan's mission. We'd green-lit his use of some of the early capital to hold training programs at the local high school and college. Out in the parking lot that day sat a huge retrofitted shipping container that served as an educational laboratory. The container classroom had all sorts of high-tech growing equipment with plants covering the walls. We watched students gingerly touch the plants and start to ask questions. Jonathan spoke to each student with the same excitement as he did when engaging with politicians.

I've always been interested in disruptive companies—those that challenge the way things have traditionally been done, particularly in areas that are critically important to our lives such as how we stay healthy, are educated, and get around. Pick the areas that matter most and that's where you'll find the biggest industries. Health care, for example, is one-sixth of the economy. Disruptive companies challenge these incumbents. They're not breaking things; they're creating a better way. That's what Jonathan is doing. He studied the current industrial food systems and found them failing on every level—supplying unhealthy food, robbing the environment of natural resources, and failing to deliver jobs and hope to the local economies. So, he asked, "Why don't we create a company that solves all these problems?"

Jonathan raised $150 million in capital as others saw the game-changing opportunity. In January 2021, in Morehead, Kentucky, one of the country's largest indoor farms began shipping tomatoes on the vine and beefsteak tomatoes to Kroger, Walmart, Publix, and other grocery chains and restaurants, with a plan to ship as much as forty million pounds of tomatoes each year just from this one farm. New facilities are being built in Richmond, Berea, and Somerset, Kentucky, with a goal to build up to twelve giant indoor farms diversifying into salad greens, berries, and other vine crops by 2025. In February 2021, Jonathan took AppHarvest public, raising $500 million.

I'll never forget watching Jonathan speak to the Forbes Under 30 Summit in 2019. The location was Detroit, and he talked poignantly about how, in a time when the cities and rural areas were often at odds, he felt common cause with the city. "What is that connection between a kid in rural Appalachia and a kid growing up in Detroit?" he asked. "The similarities kept hitting me more and more. Here in Detroit you experienced the decline of the auto industry, which had done so much to drive this country forward . . . for us in Appalachia there was one industry that the entire state was built upon and that was the coal industry." But he didn't leave it at that. Just as Detroit's decline had created an opportunity to reimagine and rebuild the city, there was a renaissance beginning in Appalachia, which is what AppHarvest was all about.

He believed in this renaissance, not yet seen or felt, and as he spoke in a quieter voice about the crisis in Kentucky, he was brought to tears just talking about his home. "When I moved back to eastern Kentucky," he said, his voice breaking, "I found that one in ten of my neighbors make less than ten thousand dollars a year. We don't talk about it . . . that's unacceptable." He paused to let the word *unacceptable* linger in the air. "The opportunity people have in this room, we've all been handed a great privilege . . . and it's hard for me to go back into those communities and think that this is the same country that we all know."

The heartache Jonathan experienced motivated his work, and that day he raised a call to action to the other young innovators gathered there. "The great companies we all talk about in twenty or thirty years are not going to be the companies that are creating some widget or gadget that you just want to sell because it's a trend and you get some marginal profit," he told them. "We have real problems. Our people and planet need to be the first two priorities. What are you doing in your community to make sure you are helping solve some of those people and planet problems that we're facing?"

From Problem to Opportunity

For a long time, our conversation about climate and sustainability was stuck in a loop of talking about it as a problem. When people are inundated by talk of a problem, especially one that feels insurmountable, they tend to tune it out. But in recent years the script has changed, and now more and more the climate situation is being viewed as an opportunity that could engage businesses, and especially bold entrepreneurs, such as Elon Musk, who has led the charge around electric vehicles and solar power, building an exceptionally valuable company (the Tesla stock hit $1 trillion in value in 2021) and inspiring a whole generation of entrepreneurs to launch climate startups.

One of these, SparkCharge, caught Revolution's attention for a seed investment. SparkCharge was creating the first mobile charging network for electric vehicles. The EV market is growing fast, with estimates that it will grow to 50 million vehicles worldwide by 2030—and that was before Russia's invasion of Ukraine triggered a new oil crisis as the United States and other countries banned the import of Russian oil. SparkCharge was early to recognize that a major barrier to purchasing EVs is the need to install charging stations, which are expensive, take up valuable real estate, and are often inaccessible and inconvenient for consumers. Creating a mobile—on the road, on demand—technology seems just what is needed to create a groundswell for electric vehicles.

As major corporations and cities are vowing zero emissions in the coming decade, there is an intensifying interest in climate technologies.

Smart Tech Changes the Temperature

Earlier, I wrote about Minneapolis and its impressive tech ecosystem, which was so effective during the pandemic. When Rise of the Rest first visited Minneapolis back in 2014, there was already evidence that this special city was attracting startups with a social purpose—nearly all the companies in our pitch competition had that in common. The winner of the competition was Deepinder Singh's 75F, a Bloomington company with a technology that regulates the temperature in offices and commercial buildings, achieving both comfort and energy efficiency. 75F has thrived since that early seed investment and has made an impact in the climate space. Rise of the Rest invested a second time when we launched our first fund, and in 2021 the company raised $28 million from investors that included Bill Gates's Breakthrough Energy, the Oil and Gas Climate Initiative, WIND Ventures, and Siemens's Next47 VC unit.

Deepinder, who refers to himself as "a startup junkie," and has been involved in six startups, grew up in India before moving to Canada and then settling in Minneapolis. The idea for 75F came from a small household dilemma that many parents face. "When my daughter was one, we moved her into her own bedroom, and she would wake up in the middle of the night crying," he said. "And I found out that it was because the temperature in her room was dropping about ten degrees at night. It was really cold. So, as a self-respecting engineer, I quit my job to fix the damn problem." He laughed, observing that all startup ventures begin with a problem, sometimes one that seems small.

Deepinder's idea might have been triggered by his daughter's discomfort, but he took it to a whole other level. Originally, he'd planned his technology for residential use, but he soon pivoted to a larger focus on office and commercial buildings. Creating the technology to regulate temperatures in buildings was a simple idea, but one that Deepinder found had a great impact, especially when applied to the vast commercial infrastructure.

"Originally it was purely a comfort play," he recalled. "I didn't have a high-level metric to consider. It wasn't a calling, just an intuitive response. If you're wearing a sweater in the summer, you probably know that something is wrong. If it's very hot in the winter, which is the case in many buildings, you're using way too much energy. Or there are some parts of a building that are too hot, and some that are too cold, and it's a problem."

As Deepinder embarked on creating algorithms to solve that problem, he learned just how important his work was to climate change. He discovered that commercial buildings were the fourth largest emitter of greenhouse gases, with "about 40 percent of greenhouse gas emissions related to buildings."

Believing there was a larger climate mission, Deepinder and his team began designing complete intelligent solutions for buildings. "Our systems make buildings smarter, make them healthier, and make them more energy efficient," Deepinder said.

During the pandemic, 75F, which has the capability to upgrade its software over the air, sent updates to the buildings to make them pandemic ready. "We introduced a concept called Epidemic Mode," Deepinder explained. "It actually complied with CDC and ASHRAE guidelines to make sure that the buildings were healthier and that the air inside was purged. We gave it to our customers for free because we'd already developed the technology that was involved, and all our customers benefitted."

With every startup Deepinder has always loved the thrill that comes from creating something new, and after a while he'd move on to the next thing. But 75F struck a different chord with him, and this company has become a long-term commitment. "For me, it's a legacy project," he said. "It answers the question, what will I see when I look back on my life?" In a concrete way he is having an impact on climate change, and "that's what keeps me going."

A Revolution in Food

The wakeup call has not just increased innovation in the energy sector. A societal push around sustainability, and a dramatic increase in interest in ESG (environment, social, and governance) investments has also created a gold rush in other sectors, including food. We backed Sweetgreen in 2013 when it was a small regional company—started by three recently graduated college friends who were looking for a better way to eat. The concept of reimagining fast food as healthy and sustainable took off in Washington, DC. Today Sweetgreen is a leader in ushering in the future of food. The company recently went public, with a $3 billion valuation.

When Revolution Growth first invested in Sweetgreen in 2013, the bulk of lunchtime options focused more on convenience than ingredients. At the time, restaurants and food tech were on the margins of most investors' minds and there was skepticism around VC-backed food concepts. But we believed in the founders, Jonathan Neman, Nicolas Jammet, and Nathaniel Ru, and their vision of a healthier way to eat.

What did we see in the then-regional salad company? Its potential to transform fast food—an industry we believed was ripe for disruption—in the same way Starbucks transformed coffee. We became convinced that fast-casual concepts would take market share from fast food, and the healthy concepts would do best of all. And the Sweetgreen founders executed brilliantly, building relationships with local farmers to get the freshest ingredients, creating food that was healthy but also full of flavor, and building a beloved brand. In addition, Sweetgreen broke out of the pack with a digital-first approach in a sector that hadn't embraced much tech innovation. In 2013, when Revolution Growth first invested, the company had already launched a mobile app that encouraged loyalty with rewards and supported mobile payments. Today, 67 percent of Sweetgreen revenue is generated from digital orders, with customers using the app for pickup or delivery and to find personalized offers, log dietary preferences, provide payment, and more. There is every indication Sweetgreen will continue to innovate, using technology to enhance customer experience.

It has been observed that the trends in food startups seem to mirror the development of tech startups. That is a natural evolution as technology becomes more integrated into our lives. As we look at the $5 trillion food market, we see a continued shift toward sustainability and healthy options. The story is being played out in a wide range of Rise of the Rest cities, and that bodes well not just for those cities, or for the founders and backers of those companies, but more broadly for the planet.

Cell Technology as a Recipe for Planet-Friendly Meals

Imagine dipping into a rich lobster chowder, full of fresh lobster meat. That would normally be an expensive proposition, as lobster retails at around $30 a pound. But this lobster, which is every bit as real as the lobster you pull from a cracked shell, was made straight from lobster cells, without having to harvest it from the wild. And this lobster doesn't originate in Maine, but in Madison, Wisconsin.

Cultured Decadence, which launched in 2020, is an example of how investors can make a bet on a more sustainable future. Cultivated meat companies are viewed as the wave of the future. In the case of Cultured Decadence, it is a vision born of sheer necessity, as the environment where these animals live naturally is under constant threat from climate change—specifically increasing ocean temperatures. Cultured Decadence is demonstrating the dispersion of innovation, and the fact that cities can be the launchpads for bold businesses that might surprise you. After all, who would have expected a seafood company to start in Wisconsin, far from the ocean?

How did the startup come about? After working in PR in China for a few years, followed by a four-year stint in the U.S. Army as an active-duty tank armor officer, John Pattison moved to New York in 2017 for business school with the dream of making money on Wall Street. The last thing on his mind was becoming an entrepreneur. One day, he was walking to class when he encountered a rep from the *Economist* handing out what he thought were hamburgers. "They said, 'Oh, it's this new thing made from plants called Beyond Meat,'" John said. "That was my gateway drug into this whole alternative protein space. I was still recruiting for banking and ended up getting a full-time job offer, but I turned it down because that experience led me to research and learn more about why people were making meat from plants. I discovered that there were two pillars of the alternative protein space. One was plant-based like Beyond Meat and the other one was cell culture, which hadn't and still really hasn't been commercialized mainstream."

John moved to the Bay Area and began to work for a cultivated meat company. There he met Ian Johnson, who had a scientific background and was working at another cultivated meat company. Together they hatched the idea for Cultured Decadence, which would focus on lobster. They brought the company home to Wisconsin—an ironic location, growing lobster in the Midwest, but John believes it's a sign of the times.

"We are literally trying to shift the entire way that you think about how food is produced without compromising on the culinary, on the food experience itself," John said. "And it's going to take time, it's going to take money. But the payoff is really what I try to talk about, and sometimes that is not just food. If we think about all the materials that come from animal products that we don't ingest as food, as a meal . . . there are multibillion-dollar industries out there, and the platform that we're building will eventually address all of them. I think in the near term, food is the best way for us to develop this technology and to come to market. But our vision goes beyond that. It goes into bio materials and maybe fabrics and other chemicals that are used in pharmaceuticals or food preservation. The people that we have onboard understand how really meaningful this could be across a variety of industries."

We had an early interest in Cultured Decadence, because cultivated meat is a promising direction for the future of food. But these kinds of startups are very time and money intensive, with technologies that can take many years to develop. So, as sometimes happens with early startups, the Cultured Decadence founders sold to Upside Foods, the first multi-species cultivated meat company, which is based in Berkeley. Madison will remain a Midwest hub for Upside, and the Cultured Decadence technologies will be integrated into Upside's existing efforts.

Can Startups Solve the Packaging Dilemma?

A world without Styrofoam is within reach. It seems like a minor step on the road to saving the planet, but it's actually a big deal. When Revolution was first introduced to TemperPack, a startup based in Richmond, Virginia, and we learned about its foray into sustainable packaging, we were interested. TemperPack engineers, manufactures, and distributes sustainable packaging products that replace single-use plastics, such as Styrofoam, with proprietary bio-based materials. The company's products are designed to help their customers eliminate the use of polystyrene and polyurethane in packaging, which accounts for 45 percent of the plastic used worldwide. In particular, Styrofoam is an environmentally poor product, normally used one time and not suitable for recycling. TemperPack's alternative is an enormous breakthrough.

It also fits the trend of the times, as people become more aware of the need for sustainable packaging. A 2019 survey showed that 77 percent of consumers believed the packaging a company uses for its online shipments should reflect its environmental values.

As e-commerce continues to grow, packaging is the new brand vehicle, and because the values that plastic represents are bad for brands, companies are serious about finding acceptable alternatives. In the corporate world, we're seeing most major companies such as Unilever, Patagonia, Nestlé, Walmart, IKEA, and Coca-Cola announcing major sustainability principles for the coming years, and a big part of that is packaging.

Governments are joining the movement as well. Regulation against the use of one-time plastics such as plastic bags and drinking straws is increasing at a state and a national level, and more than sixty countries have committed to actions that will discourage the use of plastics, which experts believe will have at least some measurable effect on consumer behavior.

With their company slogan—"We protect products with packaging that protects the earth"—TemperPack is the right startup for the times.

However, as cofounder Brian Powers is the first to admit, TemperPack came into being only after years of frustrating trial and error. He and his high school buddy James McGoff, who was studying materials engineering at McGill, first came up with the idea to create a new kind of insulation. "James had learned about a material called aerogel, which is the world's best lightest-weight insulation material," Brian said. "It's a nano material. It has been used in NASA spaceships to keep astronauts warm and other really high-end applications. It had been made cheaper recently by manufacturing. We saw the opportunity to apply it to a new application, a new product." They brought in a third partner, Charles Vincent, a materials engineer also studying at McGill.

Their first product attempt was an insulated winter jacket. They couldn't get it to work properly, and they had no fashion sense. "It was hideous," Brian acknowledged. Next up was a smart refrigerator, employing aerogel to make it more energy efficient. "No matter what we did, we couldn't get it to use less energy." They didn't give up.

"We kept dumbing it down from that. We then said, 'Okay, what if we just proved the basic concept where we take a Styrofoam box and we line the walls with aerogel, and then we compare that to a Styrofoam box without aerogel.'"

It worked. They called their invention an Airbox, and they were so excited about it they entered it in the Wharton Business Plan Competition—and got kicked out in the first round. Why? The cost. Although it was an effective cooler, at around $300, it was prohibitively expensive as a consumer leisure item.

It wasn't a total wipeout. One piece of feedback made sense—that they approach pharmaceutical companies to offer a new concept in cold chain packaging. They made some headway and were deep into R&D for this fairly narrow application when a new trend came bubbling to the surface—meal kits. Around 2015, the meal kit industry was really taking off, and when they began exploring it, they were astounded by the enthusiastic response. These companies (like HelloFresh) were sending out Styrofoam containers every single week of the year, and customers were discovering just how much they hated Styrofoam, which couldn't be recycled and felt like an insult to the planet.

"When we contacted the meal kit companies, their response was, 'When can we get it?' Immediately. They'd say, 'Here's our CEO, talk to him. How soon can you do it?' It was just a huge product market fit."

They decided to launch the company in New York City, with an assembly plant in Richmond. That didn't work out too well; they found they needed to be closer to the assembly process. Reluctantly, they decided to move to Richmond, and it was a revelation.

They were in for a pleasant surprise. Accustomed to a more hard-knock experience in New York, they found Richmond to be welcoming. The suppliers were supportive, the landlords were supportive—everyone wanted to see them succeed. They were growing fast and had very little capital, and the business community took big bets on them, giving them credit before they were credit worthy. They soon discovered that Richmond was a perfect fit for them.

Today, TemperPack has continued to thrive, backed by major investors, including Revolution. In early 2022 it closed a $140 million financing led by Goldman Sachs, and set out to further accelerate its expansion. Brian's best advice to aspiring world changers: "Don't get hung up on the idea. A lot of people wait to start something until they feel like they have a good idea, but that rarely happens. It's usually that the good idea comes after you start something, because for an idea to be good it has to be informed by real experience. Find the problem first and come up with the best idea you think of to solve that problem."

Revolution has also invested in several other promising sustainability startups. Recyclops has taken on the task of making recycling efficient and affordable. It set out to tackle a daunting challenge—creating a new model in an industry that is rife with frustration and ineffectiveness. It appeals to a population that is interested in actual sustainability, not just the facade. Those customers aren't willing to see their waste pile up in landfills. Recyclops makes it easy to recycle right from home, and it's catching on across the country. In 2021, it recycled about 1,475,465 pounds of materials.

Another of our investments is with Recurate, an Arlington, Virginia, company that deals with a different kind of recycling in the circular economy. Recurate works with companies in the fashion, electronics, and equipment industry to provide technology for customers to resell their beloved items right on the company's website. We also invested in Denver-based GoodBuy Gear, which promotes conscious shopping by enabling parents to buy and sell baby gear, so it gets reused, not thrown away.

Sustainable investing, which considers ESG factors, is a new wave that's gaining momentum. We see it in food, energy, environmental support, and other critical arenas that will make our world a safer, more livable place to be.

FOURTEEN

The United States of Possibility

At the Smithsonian's National Portrait Gallery there is a stunning 1862 oil painting titled *Men of Progress*. The artist Christian Schussele was commissioned before the Civil War to create a group portrait of eighteen American scientists and inventors who had "altered the course of contemporary civilization." Over a period of several years Schussele brought the men in to sit for portraits, which he then wove into a dramatic whole. The sober, bearded faces in the portrait belong to men like Cyrus Hall McCormick, who invented the mechanical reaper; William Thomas Green Morton, who pioneered the use of inhalable ether as an anesthetic; Charles Goodyear, who developed moldable rubber; Peter Cooper, who created the first American steam locomotive; and Elias Howe, who invented the sewing machine.

These were innovators of their era—all men, all white, mostly clustered in Northeastern cities, often working as lone wolves. They established an archetype for American invention and innovation that survived into the twentieth century, even as America expanded and became more diverse.

The twentieth century opened the door to a broader innovation landscape as inventions were geographically distributed and tied to advantages of place. George Washington Carver, the former slave who pioneered the crop rotation system that saved farms across the Midwest and South, did much of his research and experimentation at Tuskegee University in Alabama. Henry Ford built his automotive plant in Highland Park, outside of Detroit, in 1909, and cars rolled off the first assembly line there in 1913. The Wright Brothers, living in Dayton, Ohio, chose Kitty Hawk, North Carolina, to launch their first flight. Women were still left in the background, however. You might never have heard, for example, of the role of women like Grace Hopper, a Navy reserve officer who developed the first universal programming language; or Katherine Johnson, the NASA pioneer who was largely unknown until the 2016 movie *Hidden Figures* gave her a public profile.

I like to think of innovation as an inherent American quality. We often define ourselves by what we've created, beginning with a system of government that is uniquely reflected in our Constitution. We've achieved great advances in our history, but those important innovations have often been hampered by our failures to give everyone equal access to their benefits. Now, in the twenty-first century, we have an opportunity to realize our full potential, and there are signs that it is happening.

It starts with getting everyone on board. Entrepreneurial pursuits have sometimes been discouraged by parents who are more comfortable if their children choose more traditional and less risky careers. In the last generation, that picture started to change, as we saw a rise in the interest in startups.

Then the pandemic arrived, bringing new challenges and opportunities in the workplace, leading new business applications to skyrocket. The arc of innovation continues. But it requires a different playbook. A big piece of that leveling is geographic equity—the idea that every part of the nation can participate in tech-created growth. This is a core principle of Rise of the Rest. We can build on the unique strengths of different cities.

When I first started talking about Rise of the Rest nearly a decade ago, people looked at me like I'd lost it. Everybody knew all the big startup successes were in Silicon Valley, and most thought I was nutty to think cities in the middle of the country stood a real chance at competing for tech dollars and talent.

If we could convince them to join us for a Rise of the Rest bus tour, we had a shot at changing their minds. Inevitably, those who came along were surprised—and impressed—by what they experienced. They met passionate entrepreneurs building "real" companies that were poised for great success. But even then, the general sense was that it was great to see such promise in a few noncoastal cities, but it was likely more of a fluke than a trend.

The most common question journalists would ask me was to identify two to three cities on the rise that merited their attention. I always resisted, in part because it felt like asking a parent to identify their favorite child, but also because the premise of the question was wrong: it wasn't a *few* cities that were showing real promise; it was a *few dozen*.

Thankfully, the skeptics started turning into believers in the last few years, and the pandemic was clearly a tipping point. Overnight, people who would never have thought of leaving Silicon Valley found themselves working remotely from some other city. And while most thought it would be a brief adventure—maybe a few weeks, perhaps a few months—it is notable how many then decided to make a permanent change to their mailing addresses.

As a result, there is now a new awakening to the idea of discovering vibrant, well-developed startup ecosystems in unexpected towns and cities across the country. Not just the usual suspects like San Francisco, New York, and Boston, but places like Phoenix, Chattanooga, Detroit, Louisville, Baltimore, Kansas City, Salt Lake City, Omaha, Cincinnati, Green Bay, Richmond, Columbus, Atlanta, Pittsburgh, Nashville, Minneapolis, New Orleans, Memphis, Dallas, and St. Louis—and that's less than *half* of the forty-three cities our Rise of the Rest bus has visited to date. When people realize that this startup momentum exists in so many places, the response is almost universally, "Wow!"

A major takeaway of Rise of the Rest is the rapid development of collaborative networks. Everyone has a role to play, and when we express pride in American ingenuity, it is not for what people do alone—like the men in the 1862 portrait who each seemed wrapped up in his own inner world—but what they do together. In that spirit, I would offer this call to action for those who would step up to the task of building the future we envision:

For policymakers, now is the time to double down on regional economies, where the engines of progress are being harnessed to solve big problems. We can't thrive as a nation if a few people in a few places are doing really well, but most people in most places are being left behind. This is a moment, and we must seize it, to usher in a more inclusive innovation economy, which can help unite a divided nation.

For coastal venture capitalists, now is the time to expand the aperture of startups you're willing to back. Sure, it's easier to back entrepreneurs who live near you, as you can then spend more time with them, and help them grow by identifying people in your network that might be their next team members. But not all great ideas will emanate from Silicon Valley—indeed, in the internet's Third Wave the biggest opportunities will likely emerge in places far from where you live. For many of you, the pandemic opened your eyes to this, and no doubt the ability to hear Zoom pitches from entrepreneurs helped expand your deal flow. But now is not the time to go back to your comfort zone. It's time to take the next step, and show up, in person, in these rising cities, to experience firsthand what is happening. That's also the best way to help the companies you've decided to back. They also need your help in scaling, and that includes expanding your talent and partner networks to include more places.

For community and business leaders, now is the time to recognize that there is an opportunity to turn this moment into a movement and build on the recent gains. It has been great to see the shift in thinking from mayors or governors who in the past viewed "economic development" through the prism of luring a company to move their headquarters, but now recognize the real opportunity isn't in luring existing companies but in helping incubate and scale *new* companies. That's a good start, but sustained change will require a continued focus on celebrating startups, attracting investors, and winning the battle for talent.

For universities, now is the time to fulfill your role as laboratories of experimentation, workshops of innovation, and town squares where new ideas are spawned and then launched into the world. You've always been able to attract talent, but sometimes the ideas that bubbled up in your labs have failed to get into the hands of entrepreneurs who can take them and run with them, turning them into companies that can scale and succeed. Connecting to the startup ecosystems in your regions is key. So is the fight to *keep* the talent you've attracted to your cities. Ending the brain drain and unleashing a boomerang of people returning to the cities that made them is your biggest opportunity over the next decade.

For the entrepreneurs themselves, first let me say thank you. A lot of people have "good ideas," but few take that next step of turning those ideas into startups. Often, it means taking a big risk, sometimes failing, and trying again until you get it right. It's a level of boldness and commitment that sets you apart. And that's what we need more of, to write the next chapter of the American story: people who put it on the line, believing in their startup ideas, and themselves, and then building the teams that help bring those ideas to life. You are the people that will change the world—and lift up America.

Some may have called us crazy or gimmicky for driving a bus across America in search of those grand possibilities that only vigorous startup ecosystems can create. But we had to see it all for ourselves. There's no substitute for immersion in a community, even if it's only over the course of a day or two. In the process, our Rise of the Rest bus tour generates something almost magical for communities who've long felt ignored. And the inspiration works both ways. We infect one another with our ideas and our optimism.

Traveling across America helps us stay grounded and true to ourselves as we plan the future. I was intrigued a few years back to read about the writers James and Deborah Fallows's forty-eight-city tour of America in a single-engine prop plane. One of

Jim's observations resonated with me: "America thinks of itself as having a few distinct islands of tech creativity; I now see it as an archipelago of startups and reinvention." It occurred to me that you can only really see things if you look at them from a different perspective.

I could relate because in recent years my wife, Jean, and I have taken similar journeys of our own, not in a prop plane but in an RV. Rumbling along the backroads and staying in campgrounds, eating at local diners, and engaging in lively conversations with people we just met have made for the most interesting vacations we could ask for. On our most recent trip in 2019, before the pandemic, we covered 7,667 miles and twenty-six states in thirty days—a gorgeous and inspiring panorama of sights and experiences. We overnighted at Fort Abraham Lincoln State Park outside Bismarck, North Dakota. At the Montana State Fair, we feasted on a fan favorite, a Viking on a Stick, a club-shaped tube of spiced ground beef, speared onto a stick and deep-fried in batter. We drove along the Oregon Trail and followed the famed Route 66 through Colorado, New Mexico, and Texas.

Jean and I began to see those RV trips as coming home in a way, to places we'd not seen before but which always felt very familiar.

I have thought many times while on those journeys or while traveling with Rise of the Rest that, if we can only meet people where they live—find out who they are and tell them who we are, talk to them over the back fence of America—we can overcome any obstacle.

And if we can only give everybody with an idea for a new company a way to actually do something about it, no matter where they live, or what their background, or who they know—

THE UNITED STATES OF POSSIBILITY

that's what will ensure America remains the pioneering country that got us here, and preserve our lead as the most entrepreneurial nation on earth. There is indeed something special about America. It's a nation of possibility, focused more on the future than on the past.

I'm reminded of that when we celebrate the founding of our once-startup nation each year on the Fourth of July. People pour into parklands or onto beachfronts or ballfields for magnificent fireworks. They congregate in town squares and city centers. Maybe most of them are strangers, but they all gaze up at the same sky as it lights up in brilliant red, white, and blue. Thinking about that, I can feel a sense of optimism about our future. I look forward to celebrating our big 250th birthday in 2026. I hope to see you there.

Acknowledgments

After spending much of the last decade on the road, visiting cities all across the country and experiencing firsthand the entrepreneurial spark that was lighting up the nation, I knew I had to write a book chronicling my experiences. The entrepreneurs deserved to have their stories told, and the communities working so tirelessly to build a brighter future deserved recognition.

After we visited hundreds of companies in dozens of cities, it was hard to know where to start. No doubt I ended up leaving some great stories on the cutting-room floor, but I hope the overall arc of the book successfully conveys my excitement about what is happening with startups across the nation, and the dynamism that is building, unbeknownst to most Americans. My hope is this book will give *you* hope, and *America* hope, that the next chapter in the American story will be a bright one, because of the innovations now being spawned in dozens of cities.

This story would of course not be possible without the entrepreneurs themselves, who took the risk of starting companies. The odds are stacked against all entrepreneurs, because most startups fail, but the odds are particularly long in the cities that have—at least up until now—lacked vibrant, encouraging startup communities. The entrepreneurs profiled in this book, and the many, many more I've met, were undaunted, and their courage and passion inspire me.

It also wouldn't have been possible without Revolution's Rise of the Rest team. I'm grateful for the tireless leadership of managing partners David Hall and Anna Mason, who have taken the once-fledgling idea of Rise of the Rest and scaled it into a significant platform, backing more than two hundred companies in nearly one hundred cities. They, and their entire team, bring a passion to their work that is unparalleled, and their collective contributions to this book cannot be overestimated.

And thanks also to the broader team at Revolution, now fifty strong, that champion entrepreneurs at every stage of their journey. And to the dozens of investors who back our various funds and make everything we do possible.

This book was helped immeasurably by the handiwork of Catherine Whitney, a prolific author who agreed to curate the stories, interview the entrepreneurs, and work closely with me on the actual writing of the book. She was supported every step of the way by Tracy van Grack and Marissa Secreto, who took on the difficult task of guiding this book from its inception to its release.

Speaking of inception, this book wouldn't have gotten off the ground without the advocacy of my wife, Jean Case. She has been my biggest cheerleader for more than two decades, and she was the one who insisted that I write the book, believing it was a story that had to be told.

We then reached out to our longtime friend Bob Barnett, whose legendary work in the publishing world assured us that the book would reach a wide audience. And Bob in turn reconnected us with Simon & Schuster, which had done a great job in publishing my first book, *The Third Wave*, in 2016. Ben Loehnen, my editor for that book, had since launched his own imprint, Avid Reader Press, and the Avid team has been invaluable in birthing this book.

Lastly, I want to end where I started, thanking the entrepreneurs who are bringing ideas to life, enabling cities to rise again, and giving us hope that America can remain the most entrepreneurial nation in the world. Our country faces many challenges as we near our 250th birthday, but it is great to see that the pioneering spirit that animated the American story is alive and well, in cities all across our great nation.

Index

About the Author

Steve Case cofounded AOL, which at its peak handled nearly half of all internet traffic, was the first-ever internet IPO, and was the top-performing stock of the 1990s. As chair and CEO of Revolution, a Washington, DC–based investment firm he cofounded in 2005, Case has partnered with visionary entrepreneurs to build more than two hundred companies across the country. He is also the chair of the Case Foundation, which he established with his wife, Jean, in 1997. He lives in Virginia.